CELEBRATIONS

CELEBRATIONS

Elise Mecklinger

A
Cookbook
to
Benefit
the Canadian
Breast
Cancer
Foundation

CANADIAN CATALOGUING IN PUBLICATION DATA

Mecklinger, Elise

Celebrations: a cookbook to benefit the Canadian Breast Cancer Foundation

Includes index

ISBN 0-7715-7583-1

1. Holiday cookery. 2. Menus. I. Canadian Breast Cancer Foundation. II. Title.

TX739 M42 1998 641.5'68 C98-930961-4

This book is available at special discounts for bulk purchases by your group or organization for sales promotions, premiums, fundraising and seminars. For details contact: Macmillan Canada, Special Sales Department, 29 Birch Avenue, Toronto ON M4V 1E2. Tel: 416-963-8830.

Cover and interior design: Peter Ross / Counterpunch

Cover photo: Karen Whylie / Coyote Photos

Macmillan Canada

A Division of Canada Publishing Corporation

Toronto, Ontario, Canada

1 2 3 4 5 TRI 02 01 00 99 98

Printed in Canada

To my guys, Alan, Shawn, Jordy and Dave,
for the wisdom that you bring me.

Acknowledgments

There are many people that I would like to thank for their assistance in the production of this book.

My first set of thanks goes to my husband, Alan, and our three sons, Shawn, Jordy and David. You provide me with my favorite and most meaningful role – that of wife and mother. Your support for the lady of the house has been unconditional. You have hearts of gold.

I extend a special thanks to Michelle Levy for introducing me to Jay Hooper and Erin MacBride of the Canadian Cancer Foundation. Your enthusiasm for this project allowed me the opportunity to approach my publisher, Macmillan Canada.

I extend my sincere thanks to Alison Maclean and Jill Lambert of Macmillan Canada. Your expertise and encouragement have been invaluable.

I gratefully acknowledge the skilled contributions of Karen Whylie (the photographer), Peter Ross and Linda Gustafson of Counterpunch, my copyeditor, Eileen Koyama, and Meghan Brosseau, the marketing director at Macmillan.

Once again, thank you one and all for turning a dream into a reality.

CONTENTS

Introduction

The kitchen has always been my favourite place in the home. It is somehow both the hub of family activity and a refuge from the day's trials and tribulations – a place where there is almost always some form of spirited discussion. Indeed, when my sons arrive home from school I greet them in the kitchen, just as my mom did with me. This has taught me an important fact of life: if you feed them, they are happy.

Everyone loves a home-cooked meal, especially one made with care. Preparing even the simplest meal requires organization, so producing a meal for 12 or more people can be quite a daunting task. With many recipes to select from, ingredients to purchase and often unfamiliar utensils or techniques to understand, a preparation schedule should be created and closely followed. But if the purpose of entertaining is to have fun with friends and family, can the cook really have a good time in the face of all this work? I believe the answer is "yes."

I wrote *Celebrations* after discovering that few cookbooks are designed to assist the cook who actually enjoys the effort involved in entertaining. The book contains menus, preparation schedules and healthful recipes, in addition to presentation suggestions (and even appropriate music) for 12 very different occasions, including an informal brunch, a luncheon, après-ski, a child's birthday party and a more formal afternoon tea. You can also try any one recipe on its own.

I hope that after following the suggestions in this book you will agree that entertaining is not only manageable, but creative and gratifying as well. Add your own special touch and be sure to enjoy yourself – your family and friends will truly appreciate the effort.

I am proud to donate a portion of the proceeds from the sale of this book to the Canadian Breast Cancer Foundation (CBCF). The CBCF was established in 1986 as a non-profit organization dedicated exclusively to the support and funding of breast cancer research, education, diagnosis and treatment. It has helped women become more knowledgeable about this disease and, in doing so, has surely saved lives. It is my privilege to support a cause so vital to the health and well-being of mothers, daughters and sisters across Canada.

A COTTAGE MORNING

At peak season, when the weather is hot and sunny, the atmosphere at the cottage can be idyllic and nostalgic. When you are an adult, lazy days at the cottage are the closest you can get to reliving those special times at summer camp or on family vacations.

Cottagers are a casual and relaxed group. But be prepared: they are always hungry. Enlist their assistance in the food preparation and clean-up. A cooperative effort will ensure that everyone, including you, has an enjoyable time.

Menu

Serves 12

Crispy Peach French Toast

Banana Chelsea

Grapefruit, Avocado and Mango Medley

Mini Pancakes

Vegie Morning Pizza

Meat 'n' Potatoes Morning Pizza

Sweet Wheat Bread

Brunch Shakes

Blueberry Spread

Presentation

Set up this buffet in the kitchen or on the porch, using colourful paper napkins, plates and strong plastic cutlery. Line wicker baskets with napkins and use as cutlery caddies. Tall plastic tumblers can be used for the Brunch Shakes, and giant mugs for coffee and tea. Leave the bread on a cutting board with a bread knife and have guests slice their own. The French toast, pancakes, pizzas, Chelsea and Grapefruit, Avocado and Mango Medley can be put on their own platters. Decorate platters with orange slices and mint sprigs. Use cereal bowls for the Blueberry Spread, yogurt and maple syrup. Put out bowls of fresh berries.

For the buffet centrepiece, put a handful of glass marbles inside a decorative glass coffee pot. Fill it with water. Hold a group of yellow gerbera daisies in one hand and cut the stems, making them all one length. Place them in the coffee pot. Place limes, lemons and oranges decoratively around the base of the coffee pot.

I recommend *Greatest Hits, Volume 1*, by Earth, Wind and Fire, *Summer in Paradise* by the Beach Boys and *The Divine Miss M* by Bette Midler as musical background.

Preparation Schedule

Call your brunch for noon so that you have enough time to complete your preparation. To save time in the morning, I always measure out the dry ingredients for each recipe the night before.

The Day Before

1. Prepare Blueberry Spread and refrigerate.
2. Prepare the dressing for the Grapefruit, Avocado and Mango Medley and refrigerate.
3. Sauté the vegies for the Vegie Morning Pizzas and make the sausage-potato mixture for the Meat 'n' Potatoes Morning Pizzas. Refrigerate.

That Day

1. Proof the two yeasts (for the Banana Chelsea and the Sweet Wheat Bread).
2. Prepare Brunch Shakes and refrigerate.
3. Make doughs and let rise for 1 hour. Preheat oven to 400°F.
4. Assemble Grapefruit, Avocado and Mango Medley. Refrigerate.
5. Assemble Sweet Wheat Bread and bake for 30 minutes.
6. Assemble Crispy Peach French Toast and set aside.
7. Assemble Banana Chelsea. Take bread out of the oven. Lower heat to 350°F. Bake Chelsea on upper rack for 20 to 25 minutes and French toast on lower rack for 25 minutes.
8. Assemble Vegie Morning Pizzas and Meat 'n' Potatoes Morning Pizzas. Place them on cookie sheets and set aside.
9. Remove Chelsea from the oven.
10. Make pancake batter.
11. Make glaze and spread over Banana Chelsea.
12. Remove French toast from the oven. Raise heat to 450°F.
13. Bake pizzas for 8 minutes.
14. Make pancakes.

Crispy Peach French Toast

In France, French toast is known as *pain perdu* because the bread disappears when it is soaked in eggs and milk. This low-fat version has a surprise inside and will serve 12.

½ cup	white sugar
1½ tsp	cornstarch
½ cup	water
¼ cup	orange juice
1	cinnamon stick
1 tsp	grated lemon zest
1 cup	sliced fresh peaches
2	unsliced loaves bread (challah, whole-wheat or multigrain), cut into 1½-inch slices.
2 cups	1% or 2% milk
3 eggs or	4 egg whites and 1 whole egg
1 tsp	vanilla
½ cup	brown sugar
½ cup	all-purpose flour
½ cup	low-fat margarine
¼ cup	white sugar
¼ cup	graham cracker crumbs
¼ cup	granola
½ tsp	ground cinnamon
2 cups	low-fat vanilla or cappuccino yogurt OR 2 cups low-fat plain yogurt mixed with 1 tbsp calorie-reduced maple syrup

1. Preheat oven to 350°F.
2. Whisk together sugar and cornstarch in small saucepan.
3. In a small bowl, mix together water and orange juice. Over low heat gradually whisk liquid into sugar mixture. Continue blending until sugar is dissolved. Add cinnamon stick and lemon zest and simmer for 2 minutes.
4. Discard cinnamon stick and add peaches to mixture. Simmer for 2 more minutes. Remove from heat and set aside.
5. Discard ends of loaves of bread. To make a pocket in each slice of bread, cut a 2-inch-long slit along one side of each piece of bread; each pocket should extend to within 1 inch of the other sides of the slice.
6. Spoon about 1½ tablespoons of peach mixture into the pocket of each bread slice, making sure to keep each slice intact.
7. Whisk together milk, eggs and vanilla in a large bowl. Carefully soak each slice in the milk mixture.
8. Place slices on a cookie sheet that has been sprayed with cooking spray.

9. In the work bowl of a food processor, place brown sugar, flour, margarine, white sugar, graham cracker crumbs, granola and cinnamon. Process for 15 seconds or until crumbly.
10. Sprinkle brown sugar mixture evenly over bread slices.
11. Bake for 25 minutes or until topping is golden.
12. Serve with a dollop of yogurt.

Banana Chelsea

The Chelsea bun was first baked in a London bakery in the late seventeenth century. Its distinguishing feature is that it is made from a rectangular piece of dough that is rolled into a coil.This recipe produces 2 rolls, each of which turns out 9 buns.

Chelsea Dough

1 tsp	white sugar
¼ cup	warm water **OR** 1% or 2% milk (105–115°F)
1 tbsp	active dry yeast
½ cup	1% or 2% milk **OR** lukewarm water
3–3½	cups all-purpose flour
⅓ cup	white sugar
½ tsp	ground cinnamon
½ tsp	salt
¼ tsp	grated orange zest
½ cup	cold butter **OR** stick-type low-fat margarine cut into chunks
2 eggs **OR** 1 whole egg and 2 egg whites	

Filling (enough for 2 rolls)

2 cups	mashed banana (2 or 3 bananas)
1 cup	raisins
4 tbsp	brown sugar
2 tbsp	ground cinnamon

Glaze

1 cup	frozen orange juice concentrate
2 tsp	white sugar

1. To make dough, in a small bowl, dissolve sugar in warm water. Sprinkle yeast over the water. Leave the yeast mixture in a warm place to proof for 8 to 10 minutes or until bubbles appear.
2. In a small saucepan, heat milk until boiling over medium-high heat. Let cool until lukewarm.

3. Place 3 cups of the flour, sugar, cinnamon, salt and orange zest in a large mixing bowl. Stir with a wooden spoon until well combined. Cut butter into the dry ingredients with a pastry blender, or with two knives until the mixture resembles coarse oatmeal.
4. Make a well in the centre of the ingredients. Pour the yeast, eggs and milk into the well. Gradually add the dry ingredients and mix with a wooden spoon until a smooth ball forms, adding the remaining ½ cup flour, if necessary. Note: If using a food processor or an electric mixer, proof the yeast, heat the milk and then place dry ingredients in work bowl. Process or blend for 15 seconds, using the metal blade for the food processor or the dough hook for the electric mixer. Add butter and process or blend for another 15 seconds or until mixture is crumbly. Add yeast, eggs and milk and continue to process or blend until mixture forms a smooth ball.
5. Turn dough onto a lightly floured surface. Put flour on your hands and knead the dough for 5 minutes or until dough is shiny and elastic.
6. Place dough in a greased large bowl. Cover with a tea towel and let rise until double in bulk, about 1½ hours.
7. Punch down dough. Cut dough in half.
8. To make filling, mix all ingredients together with a fork. Set aside.
9. Preheat oven to 350°F.
10. On a floured surface, roll half the dough into a 9- x 12-inch rectangle.
11. Spread filling over the dough. Roll up jelly-roll style and pinch edge to seal.
12. Cut the roll into nine pieces and place cut side down in a 10- x 10-inch baking pan that has been sprayed with cooking spray.
13. Cover pan with tea towel and let rise for about 1 hour.
14. Bake for 20 to 25 minutes or until golden.
15. To make glaze, in a small saucepan heat orange juice concentrate over medium heat until melted.
16. Whisk sugar into juice and blend until dissolved.
17. Using a pastry brush, spread glaze over buns.

Grapefruit, Avocado and Mango Medley

This attractive dish provides a light and refreshing taste to the menu. It will yield 12 small portions.

5 cups	torn mixed greens
1	large pink grapefruit, peeled and sectioned
1	large avocado, halved, pitted, peeled and thinly sliced
1	mango, halved, pitted, peeled and thinly sliced
1 cup	fresh raspberries

Dressing

½ cup	orange juice
¼ cup	grapefruit juice
2 tbsp	liquid honey
1 tbsp	olive oil
1 tsp	grated orange zest
1 tsp	minced fresh ginger

1. In a small bowl, whisk together dressing ingredients until well blended.
2. Place greens in a large mixing bowl and toss with vinaigrette. Line serving platter with greens.
3. Create an attractive display on top of the greens by alternating the grapefruit, avocado and mango slices. Scatter the raspberries over top.

Mini Pancakes

If children are part of your guest list, substitute chocolate chips for the dried apricots and dates in this recipe, which should yield 10 to 12 pancakes.

1 cup	buttermilk	½ tsp	salt
½ cup	fat-free plain yogurt	¼ cup	chopped dried apricots
1	egg	¼ cup	chopped dates
2	egg whites	4 tsp	low-fat margarine for cooking
1 tsp	vanilla	1 cup	calorie-reduced maple syrup, heated
1¾ cups	all-purpose flour		
3 tsp	baking powder		

1. In a large mixing bowl, whisk together buttermilk, yogurt, egg, egg whites and vanilla.
2. In another bowl, mix together flour, baking powder and salt.
3. With a wooden spoon, add dry ingredients to liquid mixture and mix until just blended. Add apricots and dates to pancake batter.
4. Transfer batter to a large measuring cup.
5. In a large skillet, heat about 1 tsp of the margarine over medium heat. Pour approximately 2 tbsp of the batter into skillet to form a small pancake. Repeat until skillet is full; you should be able to cook three pancakes at once.
6. Cook for 1 to 2 minutes or until bubbles appear on first side; carefully flip over with spatula and cook for an additional 40 seconds or until golden. Makes about 10 to 12 mini pancakes.
7. Serve with heated maple syrup.

Vegie Morning Pizza

Pizza is making its debut in the morning. This recipe makes 8 servings.

4	flour tortillas (each 6 inches)
1 tsp	low-fat margarine
¼ cup	chopped fresh mushrooms
¼ cup	diced green pepper
1	diced green onion
1 tsp	minced fresh basil
1 cup	prepared salsa
1 cup	mixture shredded low-fat mozzarella and cheddar cheeses
4	eggs
1 tbsp	minced fresh parsley

1. Preheat oven to 450°F.
2. Place tortillas on large baking sheet that has been sprayed with cooking spray. Set aside.
3. In large skillet, heat margarine over medium heat. Sauté mushrooms, green pepper and green onion for 2 minutes or until softened. Sprinkle with basil.
4. Spread one-quarter of the salsa on each tortilla. Top with one-quarter of the cheese.
5. Spread one-quarter of the mushroom mixture on each tortilla.
6. Make a well in the centre of the mixture and carefully crack one egg over each pizza.
7. Bake for approximately 8 minutes or until eggs reach desired degree of doneness.
8. Remove from oven and sprinkle each pizza with parsley. Cut pizzas in half before serving.

Meat 'n' Potatoes Morning Pizza

A heartier pizza for the real man (or woman). Cutting each one in quarters will yield 16 appetizer portions and let everyone have a taste.

4	flour tortillas (each 6 inches)	1	green onion, cut in ¼ inch dice
4 cups	water	½ tsp	minced fresh garlic
2	chicken or veal sausages (¼ lb each)	1 cup	prepared salsa
1 tsp	low-fat margarine	1 cup	mixture shredded low-fat mozzarella and cheddar cheeses
1	large boiled potato, peeled and cut in ¼-inch dice	4	eggs
		1 tbsp	minced fresh parsley

1. Preheat oven to 450°F.
2. Place tortillas on a large baking sheet that has been sprayed with cooking spray. Set aside.
3. In a medium saucepan, bring water to a boil over medium-high heat. Prick sausages with a fork in several places. Boil for 2 minutes. Remove from saucepan and slice into ¼-inch rounds.
4. In a large skillet, heat margarine over medium heat. Add sausage and sauté for 2 minutes. Add potato, green onion and garlic and sauté for 2 more minutes or until green onion is softened.
5. Spread one-quarter of the salsa on each tortilla. Top with one-quarter of the cheese.
6. Spread one-quarter of the sausage mixture on each tortilla.
7. Make a well in the centre of the mixture and carefully crack one egg over each pizza.
8. Bake for approximately 8 minutes or until eggs reach desired degree of doneness.
9. Remove from oven and sprinkle each pizza with parsley. Cut each pizza into quarters.

Sweet Wheat Bread

There is nothing as appetizing as fresh bread hot from the oven. Have no fear. It is actually quite simple to prepare and yields about 8 to 12 slices.

1 tsp	white sugar	1 tsp	salt
½ cup	warm water (105–115°F)	¾ cup	1% or 2% milk plus 1 tbsp
1 tbsp	active dry yeast	¼ cup	brown sugar
2 cups	whole-wheat flour	1 tbsp	low-fat margarine
1 cup	all-purpose flour	1	egg white

1. Dissolve white sugar in warm water. Sprinkle yeast over top and let stand in a warm place for 8 to 10 minutes or until bubbles have appeared on top.
2. Place whole-wheat and all-purpose flours and salt in a large mixing bowl. Stir with a wooden spoon until well combined.
3. Make a well in the centre of the flour mixture. Pour in yeast and mix together with a wooden spoon until well blended.
4. In a small saucepan, heat ¾ cup of the milk over medium heat. Add brown sugar and margarine. Stir until sugar has dissolved and margarine has melted.
5. Add milk mixture to flour mixture and mix until mixture forms a smooth ball.
6. Turn dough onto a lightly floured surface. Put flour on your hands and knead the dough for 3 minutes or until the dough is shiny and elastic.
7. Place dough in a greased large bowl. Cover with a tea towel and let rise for about 1 hour or until dough has doubled in bulk.
8. Preheat oven to 400°F.
9. Punch down dough; let rise again if you have time. When ready to bake, shape dough into a loaf and place in an 8- x 4-inch loaf pan that has been sprayed with cooking spray.
10. Combine egg white and remaining 1 tbsp milk and brush over dough. Bake for 30 minutes or until browned on top.

Brunch Shakes

This recipe serves 2. Make sure to adjust your ingredients appropriately for the number of guests. For a Cantaloup Cocktail, substitute 1 cup cut-up cantaloup for the berries, and 3/4 cup orange juice for the milk.

Banana Berry Smoothie

1	medium banana
1 cup	fresh cranberries, raspberries OR strawberries
3/4 cup	skim milk OR low-fat plain yogurt
1 tbsp	liquid honey
2	ice cubes

Place all ingredients in a blender and blend until smooth.

Flour Power

Originally the word *flour* was the same as the word *flower*. When grain was milled, the most highly valued part, the meal, was characterized as the "flower."

All-purpose flour – Made from wheat flour, it is ideal for baking because of its higher gluten and protein content. The unbleached variety has greater nutritional value.

Specialty flours – Because they are lower in gluten, these types of flour must be combined with all-purpose flour to give dough elasticity.

VARIETIES INCLUDE –

Barley – used in unleavened baked goods
Oat – used in cereals and breads
Potato – used as a thickening agent
Rice – used in unleavened baked goods and noodles
Rye – used in combination with wheat flour for baking
Soy – used in combination with wheat flour for baking

Blueberry Spread

Give your everyday cream cheese a little lift. This recipe should provide enough spread for about a dozen bagels.

2 cups	low-fat cream cheese
1 tsp	grated orange rind
½ tsp	ground cinnamon
1 cup	fresh blueberries

1. In a small bowl, whisk together cream cheese, orange rind and cinnamon.
2. Gently fold blueberries into cream cheese mixture with a wooden spoon, trying not to crush the blueberries.

Berried Treasure

Delightful in pies, tarts and sauces but most impressive on their own, berries are nature's gift to the snack category.

Blackberries – Dark purple or black in colour, they are particularly good in cobblers.

Blueberries – Purplish blue in colour, they are used extensively in jams, in pies and on top of cheesecakes.

Boysenberries – Dark red to almost black in colour, they are a cross between loganberries and raspberries.

Cranberries – Red in colour, firm in texture and sour in taste, their most notable use is in the sauce that accompanies roast turkey.

Gooseberries – Small, sour and green in colour, they are sometimes used in preserves.

Huckleberries – Small and dark blue in colour, they resemble blueberries.

Loganberries – Purplish red in colour, they are a cross between blackberries and raspberries.

Raspberries – Small and red in colour, they are widely used in jams, jellies and pies.

Strawberries – Red in colour and cone shaped, they are delicious on their own.

LADIES WHO LUNCH

There are all sorts of reasons for ladies to get together: business meetings, playgroups with the children, charity luncheons, study groups or simply to enjoy each other's company.

Lunch should be something to look forward to – a welcome break in the day. Don't ever believe the lady who says that she doesn't eat lunch. As long as the menu comprises a variety of textures, colours and tastes – and a fat and calorie content that is guilt-free – she'll be there and she'll bring her friends.

Although these recipes were written to serve 12, you could probably feed a small army with the leftovers.

Menu

Serves 12

A Crostini Selection:

Broccoli Garlic Purée and Roasted Tri-coloured Peppers

Grilled Eggplant, Purple Onion and Goat Cheese

Tortilla Party Sandwiches:

Chicken and Mango Salsa

Smoked Salmon, Low-fat Cream Cheese and Dill

Caesar Salad and Sun-Dried Tomato

Herb-Crusted Salmon with Caramelized Onions and Shallots on a Bed of Mesclun Greens

Couscous with Rapini, Pine Nuts and Feta

Spinach-Laced Breadsticks

Chocolate Raspberry Pavlova

Cinnamon Snaps

Presentation

The Tortilla Party Sandwiches can form an attractive display. Lay the middle pieces on a flat serving tray. Arrange the end pieces, cut side down, as a border. Arrange the crostini on a large platter lined with curly endive lettuce leaves.

A wide oval platter can be used for the Herb-Crusted Salmon. The couscous can be served in a large bowl. For a whimsical touch, serve them in hollowed-out purple cabbages or offer individual portions in hollowed-out tomatoes or red peppers. Adorn platters with scattered edible flowers such as violets, hollyhocks and nasturtium. Serve the breadsticks in a vase.

Serve the Pavlova on a big, round cake platter, leaving enough of a margin for decoration with fresh berries and mint sprigs or dried apricots and banana chips. Tip a small basket or bowl on its side and have the Cinnamon Snaps spilling out of it. Bowls of berries and cut-up melon would complete this buffet.

Even though there is already a lot happening on this table, you may want to construct a centrepiece. Bundle together sprigs of purple basil, green basil, rosemary and tarragon. Secure each herb bundle with rubber bands. Set aside. Pile a pedestal-style cake server with a variety of fruits: apples, pears, oranges, green grapes. Tuck herb bundles around the fruit to create a border. Scatter some short-stemmed carnations, chrysanthemums or lilies over the fruit.

Since Ladies Who Lunch generally represent the baby boomer generation, it would seem appropriate that the music accompanying their lunch should have a nostalgic and sentimental touch. I would choose Carole King's *Tapestry*, James Taylor's *Sweet Baby James* and Laura Nyro's *Eli and the Thirteenth Confession.*

Preparation Schedule

Two Days Before

Make Cinnamon Snaps. Place in airtight container.

The Day Before

1. Prepare the eggplant for the crostini.
2. Make and refrigerate the Broccoli Garlic Purée.
3. Make and refrigerate Chicken Marinade, Mighty Caesar Dressing and two batches of Vegie Vinaigrette.
4. Make and refrigerate Yogurt Mustard Dressing, Herb Crust for the salmon and Yogurt Raspberry Sauce for the Pavlova.
5. Marinate the eggplant and purple onion, goat cheese and chicken in their respective vinaigrettes. Refrigerate.
6. Make Basic Crostini. Place in an airtight container.
7. Make Mango Salsa. Refrigerate.
8. Steam the spinach and sauté with onion and garlic for the Spinach-Laced Breadsticks. Refrigerate.
9. Grill the tri-coloured peppers and the chicken. Refrigerate.

That Day

1. Preheat oven to 275°F. Assemble Pavlova and bake for 1½ hours.
2. Proof the yeast for the pizza dough.
3. Rub Herb Crust on the salmon and place in the baking dish.
4. Make the pizza dough and let it rise.
5. Assemble the Tortilla Party Sandwiches and refrigerate. Remove Pavlova from the oven and raise temperature to 400°F.
6. Prepare caramelized onions and shallots. Bake for 20 minutes, drizzle with vinegar and bake for 30 more.
7. Meanwhile, steam rapini, halve olives and make couscous. Assemble Couscous with Rapini, Pine Nuts and Feta.
8. Make Spinach-Laced Breadsticks. Set aside.
9. Remove onions and shallots from the oven and bake the salmon for 15 to 20 minutes.

10. Cut up the Tortilla Party Sandwiches and arrange on platters.
11. Remove salmon from the oven. Reduce heat to 350°F. Bake Spinach-Laced Breadsticks for 12 to 15 minutes.
12. Assemble and bake crostini.
13. Assemble Pavlova.
14. On a large platter, arrange salmon, onions and shallots over mesclun greens.

A Crostini Selection

The name "crostini" comes from the Italian word *crosta*, meaning crust. Crostini are small rounds of toasted bread topped with various assortments of vegies, pastes, pâtés or cheeses. Each recipe makes 12 crostini.

Basic Crostini

1	baguette (8 oz) cut diagonally into ½-inch slices
2 tbsp	olive oil

1. Preheat oven to 400°F or heat up the barbecue.
2. Brush bread slices with olive oil and place on an ungreased baking sheet.
3. Bake, uncovered, for 7 minutes or until slices are golden and crispy. OR grill each side on the barbecue for about 2 minutes.
4. At this point, the crostini can be cooled, covered and stored for up to 1 day.

Crostini with Broccoli Garlic Purée and Roasted Tri-coloured Peppers

2	heads garlic, unpeeled
2 tbsp	olive oil
½ cup	low-fat chicken broth
3 cups	cooked broccoli florets
1	medium red pepper
1	medium orange pepper
1	medium yellow pepper
1	recipe Basic Crostini (see p.21)
¼–⅓ cup	freshly grated Parmesan cheese

1. Preheat oven to 400°F.
2. Cut ¼ inch off the top (not the root end) of each head of garlic. Remove papery outer skins.
3. Place heads, cut side up, in a small, ungreased baking dish. Drizzle oil over garlic. Pour broth into bottom of dish.
4. Bake, uncovered, for 40 to 45 minutes or until garlic appears shrivelled.
5. Squeeze contents of each clove into the work bowl of a food processor.
6. Add broccoli and remaining soup from the baking dish. Process for 10 seconds or until puréed.
7. Remove cores and seeds from each pepper. Cut each pepper in half lengthwise; cut each piece in half again lengthwise.
8. Place each piece directly on the barbecue grill or on a baking sheet that has been sprayed with cooking spray. Grill or bake until the skins are charred black, about 2 to 3 minutes. Peel off black skin and discard. Cut into ¼-inch slices.
9. Brush each crostini with approximately 1 tbsp broccoli purée. (You may have purée left over. Use later as a pasta sauce.)
10. Top with slices of red, yellow and orange pepper. (Remaining slices can be used in a salad, in pasta or as a pizza topping.)
11. Sprinkle each crostini with 1 tsp Parmesan cheese. Place on ungreased baking sheet and bake, uncovered, for 2 minutes or until cheese melts.

Crostini with Grilled Eggplant, Purple Onion and Goat Cheese

1	small eggplant, peeled and cut into twelve ½-inch rounds
1	small purple onion, cut into 12 slices
1	small log goat cheese (4.5 oz)
1 recipe	Basic Crostini (p.21)

Vegie Vinaigrette

2 tbsp	balsamic vinegar
2 tsp	minced fresh garlic
½ tsp	salt
½ tsp	pepper
⅓ cup	olive oil

1. Stack slices of eggplant in three piles on a plate. Place a sheet of wax paper over the slices. Place a heavy object (such as a can of soup or beans) on top. Let sit for 2 hours while the bitter juices drain from the eggplant. Wash slices and pat dry.
2. To make vinaigrette, in a small mixing bowl whisk together vinegar, garlic, salt and pepper. Add oil gradually, whisking until well blended.
3. In a large mixing bowl, stir together the eggplant slices and one-third of the vinaigrette.
4. Add onion slices to eggplant mixture. Blend in another third of the vinaigrette.
5. Cut goat cheese log into 12 rounds. Place in a shallow baking dish. Pour remaining vinaigrette over cheese. Let sit for 15 minutes.
6. On a hot barbecue, grill eggplant and onion slices for 2 minutes per side OR place eggplant and onion slices on a cookie sheet and broil for 2 minutes per side.
7. Preheat oven to 400°F.
8. Place crostini on an ungreased cookie sheet. Place one eggplant slice and one onion slice on each crostini. Carefully place a goat cheese slice on top.
9. Bake, uncovered, for approximately 2 minutes or until cheese melts OR place crostini directly on the barbecue and grill for 1 minute or until cheese melts.

Tortilla Party Sandwiches

Party sandwiches are addicting little treats – before you know it you've eaten far too many. Each recipe makes 9 party sandwiches.

Chicken and Mango Salsa Sandwiches

4	boneless skinless chicken breasts (about 1 lb)
3	flour tortillas (each 10 inches)

Chicken Marinade

¼ cup	lemon juice
2 tsp	minced fresh garlic
½ tsp	ground cumin
½ tsp	paprika
½ tsp	pepper
½ tsp	cayenne
½ tsp	salt
¼ cup	olive oil

Mango Salsa

1½ cups	mango cut in ¼ inch cubes
¼ cup	cubed tomatoes
¼ cup	thinly sliced green onions (green part removed)
2 tbsp	cubed green pepper
2 tbsp	lemon juice
2 tbsp	orange juice
1 tbsp	fresh minced parsley
1 tsp	minced seeded jalapeño pepper
1 tsp	minced fresh mint

1. To make marinade, in a small bowl whisk lemon juice, garlic, cumin, paprika, pepper, cayenne and salt together with a wire whisk. Slowly whisk in the oil until well blended.
2. Place chicken in a shallow, ungreased baking dish. Pour marinade over chicken. Cover and refrigerate for a few hours, turning chicken over occasionally.
3. Grill on barbecue over medium heat for about 5 minutes on each side or until no longer pink inside OR sauté chicken in a large skillet coated with cooking spray for about 5 minutes per side.
4. Cut chicken into thin diagonal slices.
5. Combine salsa ingredients in a large bowl.
6. Add chicken to the bowl of salsa and combine.
7. Divide chicken mixture among tortillas.
8. Roll up each tortilla and wrap in plastic wrap. Once all tortillas are rolled, cover them with a damp tea towel and refrigerate for a few hours before cutting each one into thirds.

Smoked Salmon, Low-fat Cream Cheese and Dill Sandwiches

¾ cup	low-fat cream cheese
3	flour tortillas (each 10 inches)
2 tbsp	minced fresh dill
1 lb	smoked salmon

Yogurt Mustard Dressing

¼ cup	fat-free plain yogurt
1 tbsp	Dijon mustard
2 tsp	lemon juice
1 tsp	white sugar

1. Whisk dressing ingredients together in a bowl.
2. Spread equal amounts of cream cheese on the tortillas.
3. Drizzle equal amounts of dressing over top.
4. Sprinkle equal amounts of dill over top of the dressing.
5. Divide smoked salmon into three portions and place on top of tortillas.
6. Roll up each tortilla. Wrap in plastic wrap. Once all tortillas are rolled, cover them with a damp tea towel and refrigerate for a few hours before cutting into thirds.

Caesar Salad and Sun-Dried Tomato Sandwiches

Everyone's favourite, the Caesar salad, becomes a sandwich filling in this recipe, but you could serve it on its own any time.

1	head romaine lettuce, torn into bite-sized pieces
3	flour tortillas (each 10 inches)
½ cup	drained oil-packed sun-dried tomatoes

Mighty Caesar Dressing

½ cup	lemon juice
¼ cup	low-fat chicken broth
1½ tbsp	minced fresh garlic
1 tsp	Dijon mustard
1 tsp	anchovy paste
1 tsp	Worcestershire sauce
½ tsp	salt
½ tsp	pepper
2 drops	Tabasco
¼ cup	freshly grated Parmesan cheese
¼ cup	olive oil

1. To make dressing, place lemon juice, broth, garlic, mustard, anchovy paste, Worcestershire sauce, salt, pepper and Tabasco in work bowl of food processor. Blend for 10 seconds. While machine is running, pour in Parmesan cheese and olive oil and process for another 10 to 20 seconds.
2. Toss lettuce with half the dressing. (Reserve remaining dressing for other use.) Divide salad among the three tortillas.
3. Place sun-dried tomatoes on top of salad.
4. Roll up each tortilla. Wrap each one in plastic wrap.
5. Gather together all the tortillas and wrap in a large damp tea towel. Refrigerate for at least one hour.
6. Just before serving, cut each tortilla into thirds.

Spice Rubs

Although the name suggests some special spa treatment, spice rubs are low-fat, flavourful ways to perk up your barbecue repertoire. For the best effect, leave rub on overnight. These rubs are enough for approximately one pound of meat, fish or poultry.

Cajun Rub

(for beef, chicken, fish and seafood)

2 tbsp	paprika
1 tbsp	garlic powder
1 tbsp	onion powder
2 tsp	salt
1½ tsp	dried thyme
1½ tsp	cayenne
1 tsp	white sugar
1 tsp	dried oregano

Jamaican Jerk Rub

(especially good with chicken)

2 tsp	curry powder
2 tsp	paprika
1½ tsp	ground allspice
1 tsp	ground cumin
1 tsp	dried thyme
½ tsp	ground cinnamon
½ tsp	ground ginger
½ tsp	salt
½ tsp	pepper
⅛ tsp	ground cloves
¼ tsp	cayenne

Indian Rub

(for fish, chicken or lamb)

2 tsp	ground coriander
1½ tsp	brown sugar
1½ tsp	ground cumin
1 tsp	ground cinnamon
½ tsp	salt
½ tsp	pepper
¼ tsp	cayenne

Combine ingredients and store in an airtight container.

Herb-Crusted Salmon with Caramelized Onions and Shallots on a Bed of Mesclun Greens

This versatile dish works well as a main course for the family dinner. This recipe makes 9 servings.

1	salmon fillet (about 2 lb)
2 cups	shallots, peeled
2	small purple onions, thinly sliced
1	head garlic, papery outer skin removed
½ cup	low-fat chicken broth
¼ cup	olive oil
	Salt and pepper
2 tbsp	brown sugar
2 tbsp	balsamic vinegar
6 cups	mesclun greens
1	recipe Vegie Vinaigrette (p.23)

Herb Crust

3 tbsp	minced fresh parsley
3 tbsp	dry breadcrumbs
2 tbsp	minced fresh basil
2 tbsp	low-fat chicken broth
2 tbsp	olive oil
1 tbsp	minced fresh garlic
½ tsp	salt
½ tsp	pepper

1. Preheat oven to 400°F.
2. In a small bowl, whisk together Herb Crust ingredients.
3. Rub over top of salmon and place fillet skin side down on a baking sheet that has been sprayed with cooking spray.
4. Bake, uncovered, for 15 to 20 minutes or until fish flakes easily with a fork and flesh is opaque.
5. Whisk together chicken broth and olive oil. Pour over shallots, onion and garlic.
6. Place shallots, onion and garlic on a cookie sheet that has been sprayed with cooking spray. Keep garlic separate. Sprinkle brown sugar over the shallots and onions.
7. Bake, uncovered, for 20 minutes or until sugar has melted and shallots and onions are wilted.
8. Drizzle with balsamic vinegar and bake for another 30 minutes. Place shallots and onions in a large mixing bowl.

9. Add garlic, squeezing contents of each clove into the bowl, and mix thoroughly.
10. Mix mesclun greens with vinaigrette. Place on large oval platter.
11. To divide salmon into 9 portions, cut three slices, each about 2 inches wide, off the tail end of the fillet. Halve the remaining fillet lengthwise and cut each half into three slices widthwise, each about 2 inches wide, to create six more pieces. Carefully place salmon pieces on top of the greens and fit them together to resemble the original fillet.
12. Surround the salmon with the caramelized onion mixture.

Couscous with Rapini, Pine Nuts and Feta

Try serving this couscous in a large, leafy, hollowed-out cabbage. This recipe yields 8 to 12 portions.

2½ cups	vegetable broth	⅓ cup	nicoise olives, halved and pitted
2 cups	couscous	¼ cup	finely chopped fresh parsley
2 tsp	olive oil	⅓ cup	crumbled feta cheese
¼ cup	pine nuts		
2 cups	chopped rapini, stems discarded		

1. In a medium saucepan, bring vegetable broth to a boil. Add couscous and stir. Remove from heat and let stand, covered, for 5 minutes or until tender. Fluff with a fork.
2. In a small skillet, heat oil over medium heat and sauté pine nuts for 2 minutes or until golden.
3. Place rapini in vegetable steamer and steam over boiling water for 3 minutes or until wilted. Rinse under cold water. Squeeze out excess moisture and coarsely chop.
4. In a large bowl, mix together couscous, rapini and pine nuts. Add olives and parsley and mix thoroughly.
5. Transfer mixture to a large serving bowl and sprinkle feta cheese over top.

Spinach-Laced Breadsticks

For variety, replace the spinach with chopped black olives or chopped sun-dried tomatoes. If you're short on time, use prepared pizza dough (½ lb). This recipe makes 12 breadsticks.

1	bunch spinach, stems removed
2 tsp	olive oil
¼ cup	finely chopped onion
1 tbsp	minced fresh garlic
1 tsp	white sugar
	Salt and pepper
1 tbsp	sesame or poppy seeds
1	egg white
1 tsp	water

Pizza Dough

2 tsp	white sugar
¾ cup	warm water (105–115°F)
1½ tsp	active dry yeast
2 tbsp	olive oil
1 tsp	salt
2 cups	all-purpose flour

1. To make pizza dough, dissolve sugar in warm water and then sprinkle yeast over the water. Leave the yeast mixture in a warm place to proof for 8 to 10 minutes or until bubbles appear.
2. Stir olive oil and salt into yeast mixture.
3. Place flour in a medium bowl. Make a well in the centre; add yeast mixture and stir with a spoon until blended.
4. Lightly flour your hands and, on a floured surface, knead the dough until it is no longer sticky, about 5 minutes. Add more flour if necessary.
5. Transfer the dough to a greased large bowl. Cover the bowl with a tea towel and let the dough rise until it has doubled in bulk, about 1 hour.
6. When the dough has risen, place it on a floured surface and punch it down. Cover it with a tea towel and let it rest for 15 to 20 minutes.
7. In a vegetable steamer, steam spinach for 2 minutes or until wilted. Rinse under cold water. Squeeze out excess moisture and coarsely chop.
8. In a large skillet, heat oil over medium heat. Add onions and garlic and sauté for 2 minutes or until softened. Add spinach and sauté for another minute. Add sugar and blend thoroughly. Sprinkle with salt and pepper to taste. Set aside.
9. Preheat oven to 375°F.

10. On a floured surface, roll out dough into a 10- x 12-inch rectangle.
11. Press spinach mixture evenly into the dough. Sprinkle with sesame seeds.
12. Cut the dough crosswise into 12 strips, each 1 inch wide. Gently twist each strip and place strips 1 inch apart on two cookie sheets that have been sprayed with cooking spray. (If you are looking to be creative, you could form these strips into different shapes such as numbers or letters.) Brush with egg white and water mixture.
13. Bake, uncovered, for 12 to 15 minutes or until browned.

Chocolate Raspberry Pavlova

Chocolate and raspberry are a sinful blend. Fortunately, this recipe is low fat – so enjoy! It will serve 12.

5	egg whites
1/8 tsp	salt
1/4 tsp	cream of tartar
1 cup	white sugar
1 1/2 tbsp	cornstarch
2 1/2 tbsp	unsweetened cocoa
1 tbsp	white vinegar
1 1/2 tsp	vanilla

Yogurt Raspberry Sauce

6 cups	fresh raspberries
1/2 cup	white sugar
1 tsp	lemon juice
3	containers (each 6 oz) of fat-free plain, raspberry or vanilla yogurt
2 tbsp	mini chocolate chips

1. Preheat oven to 275°F.
2. Using an electric mixer, beat egg whites, salt and cream of tartar together until stiff peaks form.
3. Gradually beat in sugar until glossy peaks form.
4. Sprinkle cornstarch and cocoa over top and gently fold in with a plastic spatula.
5. Gently fold in vinegar and vanilla.
6. On a foil lined cookie sheet that has been sprayed with cooking spray, mound the meringue into a 10" circle.
7. Bake for 1 1/2 hours. Let cool. Using a large metal spatula, transfer to a serving platter.
8. To make sauce, in a small saucepan, bring 2 cups of the raspberries, sugar and lemon juice to a boil over medium-high heat.
9. Reduce heat to low and cook, uncovered, for another 10 minutes or until thickened.
10. In a large mixing bowl, blend together yogurt and raspberry mixture.
11. Spoon onto meringue. Arrange remaining 4 cups raspberries on top of yogurt mixture. Sprinkle with chocolate chips.

Cinnamon Snaps

Every good lunch deserves to end with a good crunch. These little treats fit the bill.

½ cup	all-purpose flour
½ tsp	ground cinnamon
5 tbsp	butter
¼ cup	white sugar
3 tbsp	light corn syrup

1. Preheat oven to 375°F.
2. In a small mixing bowl, sift together flour and cinnamon.
3. In a medium saucepan, heat butter over medium-low heat. With a wire whisk, blend in sugar and corn syrup.
4. Add flour mixture and continue stirring until well blended.
5. Place a heaping teaspoon of batter onto a cookie sheet that has been sprayed with cooking spray. With the back of a spoon, create a thin rectangle, about 6 inches long.
6. Make two more cookies, ensuring that they are at least 2 inches apart on the sheet.
7. Bake for 7 to 9 minutes or until golden brown. Let cool for about 30 seconds. Cookies should still be a little pliable.
8. Wrap each warm cookie around the handle of a wooden spoon to form a curve.
9. Repeat steps 5 to 8 to make 10 to 12 cookies.

Appetizer Variations

The following items are also good with crostini toppings. Celery stalks, hollowed-out zucchini shells and Belgian endive leaves also work well. These recipes serve 12.

Potato Skins – Slice 6 baked potatoes in half and scoop out the pulp. Brush cavities with 1 tbsp minced garlic mixed with 2 tbsp olive oil and place on a cookie sheet that has been sprayed with cooking spray. Bake, uncovered, at 475°F for 7 to 10 minutes or until golden.

Angel Hair Nests – Brush a 12-cup muffin tin with 2 tbsp olive oil mixed with 1 tbsp minced garlic. Divide 8 oz cooked angel hair pasta among the cups to create nests. Drizzle with olive oil and sprinkle with salt and pepper. Bake, uncovered, at 375°F for 12 minutes or until nests are crispy.

PIZZA PASTA PERFECTION

A pasta bar provides the perfect culinary setting for a casual get-together of friends or family, be it a birthday, a graduation, a house-warming or just a Saturday night.

Guests can pick their choice of sauce, their favourite type of pasta and the ingredients to go with it. All items are displayed in an attractive buffet. Ideally you could have a few guests cooking up specialty orders for everyone else. Everybody can participate in this interactive event.

Add a few different kinds of pizza, a Caprese salad and a sorbet bar to the menu, and your dinner for 12 is complete.

Menu

Serves 12

Pasta Bar with Selection of Sauces:

Roasted Tomato Garlic

Fagioli

Sweet Potato

Dill Yogurt

Tonnato

Puttanesca

Pesto

Pizzas:

Mushrooms, Purple Onion and Goat Cheese

Chicken, Sun-Dried Tomatoes and Artichokes

Caprese salad

Peachy Sorbet

Over the Top:

Chocolate Topping

Raspberry Swirl

Sweet Additions

Presentation

Have three bowls of cooked pasta on display – farfalle, rotini and penne. Make sure to stir a little cooking liquid into the pasta to prevent sticking.

Serve each pasta sauce in its own bowl. Display the following items in their own bowls:

cubed cooked chicken
grilled beef slices
grilled vegies, cut into bite-sized pieces: red peppers, purple onions, zucchini, potatoes
raw vegies, cut up into bite-sized pieces: tomatoes, mushrooms, green onions
fresh herbs: chopped fresh basil, chopped fresh parsley, chopped fresh oregano
cheeses: crumbled goat cheese, freshly grated Parmesan, shredded low-fat mozzarella

Assembly:

In a large skillet, heat 1/4 cup of sauce over medium-low heat. Add 2 cups of cooked pasta and stir until thoroughly coated with sauce. Add ingredients of choice and heat through for another 30 seconds. Add cheese just before serving.

Bring the pizzas out fresh from the oven. Be sure to place them on a surface that is protected from the heat.

Serve the Caprese salad on a large platter.

Since your table is already quite crowded with the pasta bar, simply fill some of the empty spaces with colourful, fresh vegetables such as red, yellow and orange peppers, eggplant and zucchini. Wash out some empty balsamic vinegar and olive oil bottles and use them as bud vases for single red roses.

After dinner is over, clear the buffet table. Scoop out the sorbet into individual portions. Place in a large trifle bowl. Place this bowl into an even larger bowl containing ice cubes. Set out the bowls of toppings close by.

Highlight the interaction among the guests with vintage Beatles albums (CDs) such as *Sgt. Pepper's Lonely Hearts Club Band, Rubber Soul, Revolver* and the *White Album*.

Preparation Schedule

To avoid falling into panic mode, prepare many items on the menu the day before. If you feel the need to take a few shortcuts, you can buy prepared pizza dough or pizza crusts and sorbet . . .

The Day Before

1. Make the sorbet(s).
2. Put each Sweet Addition in little plastic bags, all set to be placed in decorative bowls the next day.
3. Roast tomatoes, onions and garlic for Roasted Tomato Garlic Sauce.
4. Roast tomatoes, garlic and red pepper for Puttanesca Sauce.
5. While vegetables are roasting, make Dill Yogurt Sauce, Tonnato Sauce and Pesto. Store in airtight containers in the refrigerator.
6. Complete the Roasted Tomato Garlic Sauce and store in an airtight container in the refrigerator.
7. Complete Puttanesca Sauce and store in an airtight container in the refrigerator.
8. Make the Raspberry Swirl and store in an airtight container in the refrigerator.

That Day

1. Assemble ingredients for pasta bar.
    a. Grill slices of red pepper, purple onion, zucchini and little red new potatoes that have been cut in quarters. Sprinkle with salt and pepper and transfer to platter.
    b. Grill one 8-oz strip loin steak. Cut into thin slices. Transfer to platter.
    c. Cut up raw vegies and put in decorative bowls.
    d. Put pieces of cooked chicken in their own bowl.
    e. Chop up the herbs and put in little bowls.
    f. Put each kind of cheese in its own plastic bag. Transfer to bowls right before serving.
2 Proof the yeast for the pizzas.
3. Assemble Caprese salad.
4. Make the doughs and let them rise for about 1 hour.
5. Sauté the mushrooms, onions and pine nuts for the pizza and set aside.

6. Make Sweet Potato Sauce and put it in a serving bowl.
7. Make Fagioli Sauce and put it in a serving bowl.
8. Put other sauces in serving bowls.
9. Preheat oven to 475°F.
10. Boil and drain pastas and put in serving bowls.
11. Make Chocolate Topping and place in serving bowl.
12. Assemble the two pizzas. Bake one after the other for 8 to 10 minutes each.
13. Put toppings on Pizza with Chicken, Sun-Dried Tomatoes and Artichokes and bake for 8 to 10 minutes more.

Pasta Bar with Selection of Sauces

Roasted Tomato Garlic Sauce

Use this wonderfully flavourful sauce for the Pizza with Chicken, Sun-Dried Tomatoes and Artichokes (p.47). This recipe yields enough sauce for 1 pound of pasta.

2 lb	plum tomatoes, halved	1 tbsp	freshly grated Parmesan cheese
1	medium onion, quartered	1 tbsp	minced fresh basil
3	heads garlic, unpeeled, separated into cloves	1 tbsp	minced fresh oregano
		1 tbsp	tomato paste
1 tbsp	olive oil	1 tsp	white sugar
Salt and pepper		½ tsp	salt
½ cup	vegetable or low-fat chicken broth	½ tsp	pepper

1. Preheat oven to 400°F.
2. Place tomatoes, onion and garlic in an ungreased 9- x 13-inch glass baking dish. Drizzle with olive oil. Sprinkle with salt and pepper. Bake for 40 to 45 minutes or until tomatoes are shrivelled.
3. Peel tomatoes and discard skin. Place tomatoes and onions in the work bowl of a food processor. Add garlic, squeezing contents of each clove into bowl. Process for 20 seconds.
4. Add broth, cheese, basil, oregano, tomato paste, sugar, salt and pepper to the bowl and process for another 30 seconds or until blended.

Fagioli Sauce

Beans are a healthy complement to this sauce, which makes enough for about 1 pound of pasta.

2 tsp	olive oil	½ cup	vegetable or low-fat chicken broth
2 tbsp	minced fresh basil	2 cups	diced tomatoes
1½ tbsp	minced fresh garlic	¼ cup	dry white wine
1 tsp	minced fresh oregano	1 can	(14 oz) white kidney beans, drained
1	bay leaf		

1. In a large skillet, heat oil over medium heat. Add basil, garlic, oregano and bay leaf to pan. Add broth and cook for 1 to 2 minutes.
2. Add tomatoes and wine to the pan and cook for another 2 minutes or until heated through. Discard bay leaf.
3. Just before serving, add beans and heat through.

Sweet Potato Sauce

This sauce has an attractive burnt orange colour. Try serving it over 1 pound of ravioli or tortellini.

1 tsp	olive oil
1	large onion, cut in ½-inch cubes
1 tsp	minced fresh garlic
2 cups	mashed sweet potatoes (about 1½ lb)
1 tbsp	brown sugar
¼ tsp	ground cinnamon
1½ cups	vegetable or low-fat chicken broth
¼ cup	evaporated skim milk

1. In a large skillet, heat oil over medium heat. Add onion and garlic and sauté until soft, about 3 minutes.
2. Add sweet potatoes and stir for another 2 minutes or until well blended.
3. Sprinkle brown sugar and cinnamon over sweet potato mixture.
4. Raise heat to medium high. Whisk in broth and milk. Reduce heat to low and simmer for 5 minutes.
5. Pour mixture into the work bowl of a food processor. Process for 20 seconds or until puréed.

Dill Yogurt Sauce

This sauce works well for a cold pasta salad. Try using 1 pound of short noodles such as farfalle, penne or rotini.

1 cup fat-free plain yogurt
1 cup buttermilk
¼ cup loosely packed fresh dill, stems removed
1 tbsp minced fresh garlic
1 tsp lemon juice
1 tsp Worcestershire sauce

Whisk all ingredients together in a bowl.

Pasta Sauce Versatility

1. Use Roasted Tomato Garlic Sauce in lasagne.
2. Add 2 cups more broth and 1 cup cooked pasta to Fagioli Sauce to make a delicious soup.
3. Mix 2 cups cooked white rice with ½ cup Dill Yogurt Sauce to make a rice salad.
4. Add 2 cups more broth to the Sweet Potato Sauce to make a soup OR replace the broth in the Sweet Potato Sauce with melted low-fat margarine, and ¼ cup all-purpose flour, bake in a 325°F oven for 30 minutes, and you've got a side dish.
5. Replace the sweet potato in the Sweet Potato Sauce with squash or turnips.
6. Serve Puttanesca Sauce on the side of grilled grouper or sea bass, or use it as part of a filling in rolled sole or chicken breasts.
7. Stuff Pesto between the skin and the meat of chicken pieces or a whole chicken, and roast.
8. Add Pesto to dough for breadsticks before baking.

Tonnato Sauce

This sauce blends together the delicate flavours of tuna, anchovies and fresh herbs. It works well with 1 pound of pasta such as fusilli or orechiette, served at room temperature.

1½ cups	fresh basil, stems removed
1	can (7 oz) water-packed tuna, drained
½ cup	fresh parsley, stems removed
4 tbsp	fat-free mayonnaise
2 tbsp	lemon juice
2	anchovies, cut in small pieces
¼ cup	olive oil

1. Place basil, tuna, parsley, mayonnaise, lemon juice and anchovies in the work bowl of a food processor. Process for 1 minute or until blended.
2. While machine is running, add oil and process for another 20 seconds or until well blended.

Puttanesca Sauce

Literally translated, the Italian word *puttanesca* is used to describe a lady of the evening. This spicy sauce will dress up 1 pound of long noodles such as cappelli or fettucine. Serve it hot.

5	medium tomatoes, quartered	½ cup	niçoise olives, cut in ¼-inch cubes
1	head garlic, unpeeled, separated into cloves	¼ cup	green olives, cut in ¼-inch cubes
1	medium red pepper, seeded and quartered	3 tbsp	capers
1 tbsp	olive oil	2	anchovies, cut in small pieces
	Salt and pepper		

1. Preheat oven to 400°F.
2. Place tomatoes, garlic and red pepper in an ungreased 9- x 13-inch glass baking dish. Drizzle olive oil over top. Sprinkle with salt and pepper. Bake for 40 to 45 minutes or until vegies have shrivelled.
3. Place tomatoes and red pepper in the work bowl of a food processor. Add garlic, squeezing contents of each clove into bowl. Process for 1 minute or until puréed.
4. In a medium skillet, heat tomato purée over medium-low heat. Add niçoise and green olives, capers and anchovies, reduce heat to low, and cook for another 5 minutes.

Pesto

This sauce is a beautiful, fresh shade of green. Any type of noodle, such as macaroni or pappardelle, works well with this sauce. Serve it hot or cold.

- 1½ cups fresh basil, stems removed
- ½ cup fresh parsley, stems removed
- ½ cup freshly grated Parmesan cheese
- ½ cup vegetable or low-fat chicken broth
- ¼ cup fresh breadcrumbs
- ¼ cup pine nuts
- 2 tbsp minced fresh garlic
- ½ cup olive oil

Place basil, parsley, cheese, broth, breadcrumbs, pine nuts and garlic in the work bowl of a food processor. Process for 30 seconds. While machine is running, add oil and process for another 30 seconds or until well blended.

Pizzas

Pizza with Mushrooms, Purple Onion and Goat Cheese

Cut into 12 thin slices so that everyone can have a taste.

1	recipe Pizza Dough (p. 30)	½ cup	thinly sliced button mushrooms
2 tsp	olive oil	½	small purple onion, thinly sliced
1½ tsp	minced fresh garlic		
1 tsp	minced fresh oregano	2 tbsp	pine nuts
2 tbsp	low-fat chicken broth	1 cup	goat cheese

1. Preheat oven to 475°F.
2. Roll out and stretch pizza dough to fit a 16-inch pizza pan that has been sprayed with cooking spray.
3. Mix olive oil and 1 tsp of the garlic together in a small bowl. Using a pastry brush, spread mixture on pizza. Sprinkle with oregano.
4. Bake for 8 to 10 minutes or until crust is lightly browned.
5. While pizza is in the oven, in a medium skillet, heat broth over medium heat. Sauté mushrooms, onion and remaining ½ tsp garlic together for 2 minutes or until softened. Add pine nuts and cook for another minute.
6. Remove pizza from the oven and top with the mushroom mixture. Sprinkle goat cheese over top.
7. Return to oven and bake for another 8 to 10 minutes or until the crust is golden. Cut pizza into 12 pieces.

Pizza with Chicken, Sun-Dried Tomatoes and Artichokes

Cut into 12 thin slices.

1	recipe Pizza Dough (p. 30)
1 cup	Roasted Tomato Garlic Sauce (p. 39)
½ cup	chopped cooked chicken
¼ cup	chopped, drained oil-packed sun-dried tomatoes
1	small jar (6 oz) artichoke hearts, drained, each heart halved lengthwise
1½ cups	shredded low-fat mozzarella cheese

1. Preheat oven to 475°F.
2. Roll out and stretch dough to fit a 16-inch pizza pan that has been sprayed with cooking spray.
3. Spread sauce over pizza. Bake for 8 to 10 minutes or until crust is lightly browned.
4. Remove from the oven and sprinkle pizza with chicken, sun-dried tomatoes and artichoke hearts. Top with shredded cheese.
5. Return to oven and bake for another 8 to 10 minutes or until crust is golden. Cut pizza into 12 pieces.

Other Pizza Tops and Bottoms

Tops

Grilled, roasted, sautéed or leftover vegies: eggplant, zucchini, peppers, mushrooms, onions, garlic, shallots, potatoes, squash, spinach.
Raw vegies: tomatoes, scallions, arugula.
Fresh herbs: basil, rosemary, oregano and thyme.
Anchovies, capers, sardines, grilled or canned salmon and tuna, smoked salmon.
Cooked chicken, turkey, sausage, ground beef.
Pineapple chunks, fig quarters, raisins, pine nuts.
Cheeses: low-fat mozzarella, goat cheese, bocconcini, low-fat cheddar, Gruyère, ricotta.

Bottoms

Greek-style pitas, English muffins, tortillas and bagels make fast and easy dough substitutes. Add toppings and bake these pizzas in a 450°F oven for 10 minutes.

Caprese Salad

For an extra decorative touch, scatter some capers and chopped purple onion over top of this salad. Makes 12 portions.

6	large tomatoes, cut into ½-inch slices	½ tsp	salt
20	slices low-fat mozzarella cheese	¼ cup	olive oil
3 tbsp	balsamic vinegar	2 tbsp	minced fresh basil
2 tsp	minced fresh garlic	2 tbsp	chopped chives
			Pepper
		Freshly grated Parmesan cheese	

1. Overlap alternate slices of tomatoes and mozzarella cheese on a serving platter. Depending on the size of the platter, you will have two or three rows.
2. In a small bowl, whisk together vinegar, garlic and salt until blended. Gradually whisk in oil.
3. Drizzle dressing over tomatoes and cheese.
4. Scatter basil and chives over top. Sprinkle with pepper and Parmesan cheese.

Peachy Sorbet

In keeping with the “create your own” theme, a sorbet bar completes the meal. This recipe serves six, so make two batches to feed your crowd of 12. Or make one peach sorbet and one raspberry sorbet by substituting raspberries for peaches, cranberry-raspberry juice for peach nectar and crème de cassis for peach schnapps.

1½ cups	water
1½ cups	white sugar
3 cups	sliced fresh peaches
1½ cups	peach nectar
½ cup	peach schnapps

1. In a medium saucepan, heat water over medium heat. Gradually whisk in sugar and let mixture boil for 2 minutes or until sugar is dissolved.
2. Reduce heat to low. Add peaches and nectar. Simmer for 5 minutes or until peaches have become mushy.
3. Place mixture in the work bowl of a food processor. Process for 20 seconds or until puréed. With machine running, add schnapps through the feed tube. Process for another 20 seconds or until well blended.
4. Place mixture in a 9- x 13-inch glass baking dish. Cover with foil and refrigerate for a few hours.
5. Place sorbet in an ice cream maker and freeze according to manufacturer’s directions.

Over the Top

Chocolate Topping

A little extra flavour goes a long way. Drizzle this sauce over your sorbet and you'll have created a delightful experience for the tastebuds. This recipe yields 1 to 1 1/2 cups sauce.

¾ cup	light corn syrup	1 tsp	vanilla
⅓ cup	skim milk	¾ cup	white sugar
2 tsp	low-fat margarine	½ cup	cocoa powder

1. In a medium saucepan, heat corn syrup over medium-low heat. Add milk, margarine and vanilla and stir until well blended, about 2 minutes.
2. Whisk in sugar and cocoa powder and cook for another 2 minutes or until blended.

Raspberry Swirl

Blueberries or any mixture of berries also work well in this recipe. This recipe makes 1 1/2 cups.

1 cup	water
1 cup	white sugar
1 tbsp	cornstarch
2 cups	fresh raspberries
2 tsp	lemon juice

1. In a medium saucepan, heat water and sugar over medium-low heat. Whisk for 2 minutes or until mixture is clear. Whisk in cornstarch and blend for another 2 minutes.
2. Put sugar mixture into the work bowl of a food processor. Add raspberries and lemon juice and process for 1 to 2 minutes or until well blended. Strain mixture in a sieve.

Sweet Additions

Offer your guests the following items to sprinkle over their sorbet:

shelled pistachio nuts
white chocolate chips
dried banana chips
dried apple and apricot pieces
raisins
shredded coconut
broken pieces of calorie-reduced chocolate bars

Some Spicy Meatballs

Little meatballs add bite-sized delight to your pasta dish. This recipe yields from 12 to 16 meatballs.

1 tsp	olive oil	1 tsp	minced fresh garlic
½ cup	chopped onions	1 tsp	minced seeded jalapeño pepper
1½ lb	minced chicken OR veal OR lean ground beef	½ tsp	salt
½ cup	cornflake crumbs	½ tsp	pepper
¼ cup	ketchup		

1. Preheat oven to 350°F.
2. In a small skillet, heat oil over medium heat. Add onions and sauté for 2 minutes or until softened.
3. Transfer to the work bowl of a food processor and process for 15 seconds. Add chicken, cornflake crumbs, ketchup, garlic, jalapeño pepper, salt and pepper and process for 30 seconds or until well blended.
4. Wet your hands and shape mixture into 1-inch meatballs.
5. Bake on an ungreased cookie sheet for 30 to 40 minutes or until browned.

How to Make Flatbread

Transform pizza dough into this bread basket charmer. Cut it into 12 slices.

1	recipe Pizza Dough (p. 30)	1½ tbsp	sesame seeds
1 tsp	olive oil	½ tsp	coarse salt
1½ tbsp	poppy seeds		

1. Preheat oven to 375°F.
2. Place dough on a surface that has been dusted with flour. Punch down. Divide dough into four portions and cover with plastic wrap until you're ready to use them.
3. Roll out one portion at a time as thinly as possible. Peel dough off the work surface and place on a baking sheet that has been sprayed with cooking spray.
4. Brush with olive oil. Prick randomly with tines of a fork.
5. Sprinkle poppy seeds, sesame seeds and salt over flatbread.
6. Bake for about 20 minutes or until crisp and lightly browned. Cut into 12 pieces.

TEA IN THE AFTERNOON

The ritual of afternoon tea originated in England in the eighteenth century. As the usual time for dinner became later in the evening, the need for late afternoon refreshment arose.

Nowadays the afternoon tea party is the perfect setting for a birthday party, a holiday gathering, a bridal shower, even a business meeting.

Afternoon tea is paradise for someone with a sweet tooth: tarts, muffins, danishes and cookies abound. These recipes, however, are low in fat and therefore not taboo like their rich counterparts.

These recipes will feed anywhere from 12 to 24 people, depending on their sweet tooth. I have the feeling that leftovers will not go to waste.

Menu

Serves 12 to 24

Tea-Time Nachos:

Strawberry Kiwi

Lemon

Sweet Strudels

Scones:

Blueberry Buttermilk

Chocolate Peanut Butter

Chocolate Madeleines

Snowballs

Cranberry Lemon Biscotti

Little Lime Cheesecakes

Little Date Bites

Double Berry Muffin Tops

Presentation

An afternoon tea party is the perfect excuse to use fine china and silver serving pieces. Set up your buffet table with small dessert plates, cups and saucers, and teaspoons. Line silver trays and cake plates with gold or silver doilies. A silver tea service provides an elegant touch.

For the centrepiece, take a dozen seashell roses in shades of peach, shrimp pink and coral, and cut the stems to about 6 or 7 inches. Place them in a silver ice bucket or pitcher. Take six fully bloomed roses and cut the stems to 3 inches. Pour some water into a two-inch-deep china casserole dish or platter and float the roses inside it. If there is room, add some vanilla-scented floating candles. Place alongside the first arrangement.

In keeping with the elegant setting, have opera as your background music. Play Placido Domingo's *Always in My Heart, Carreras, Domingo and Pavarotti in Concert* and *The Three Tenors in Concert, 1994.*

Preparation Schedule

Fortunately, many of the items can be made in advance.

One to Two Weeks Before

1. Make Double Berry Muffin Tops. Place in an airtight container and freeze.
2. Make Little Date Bites. Place in an airtight container and freeze.

Two Days Before

1. Make Chocolate Madeleines and place in an airtight container.
2. Make Cranberry Lemon Biscotti and place in an airtight container.
3. Make Snowballs and place in an airtight container.

The Day Before

1. Make Little Lime Cheesecakes early in the day so that the cheesecake can be refrigerated for 4 hours before cutting. Cut into pieces, put them in paper muffin cups and put in an airtight container.
2. Make the two types of scones and place in an airtight container.
3. Take Double Berry Muffin Tops and Little Date Bites out of the freezer.

That Day

1. Proof the yeast for the two strudel doughs.
2. Make the cream cheese filling for Strawberry Kiwi Nachos.
3. Make the Cheese and Raisin Filling.
4. Make the doughs and let them rise for 1 hour.
5. Make the Apple Filling.
6. Make the lemon mixture for Tea-Time Nachos and refrigerate.
7. Preheat the oven to 400°F.
8. Assemble the two strudels and let rise for 1 hour.
9. Assemble the Tea-Time Nachos and bake for 5 to 7 minutes. Lower heat to 375°F.
10. Glaze the strudels and bake for 25 minutes.

11. While strudels are baking, arrange biscotti, madeleines, scones, Tea-Time Nachos, cheesecakes, muffin tops, Little Date Bites and Snowballs decoratively on platters and cake stands.
12. Cut up strudels and place on platters.

Tea-Time Nachos

The versatile tortilla makes its way to the dessert buffet. Each recipe makes 24 treats.

Strawberry Kiwi Nachos

6	flour tortillas (each 6 inches)	2 tbsp	skim milk
1 cup	low-fat cream cheese	2 tsp	lemon juice
2 tbsp plus 2 tsp	white sugar	2 tsp	ground cinnamon
2 tbsp	fat-free sour cream	24	kiwi slices
		24	strawberries, halved

1. Preheat oven to 400°F.
2. Place tortillas on two cookie sheets that have been sprayed with cooking spray.
3. Place cream cheese, 2 tbsp of the sugar, sour cream, milk and lemon juice in a mixing bowl. Using an electric mixer, beat at medium speed until well blended.
4. Divide mixture among tortillas, spreading it out evenly.
5. Mix remaining 2 tsp sugar and cinnamon in a small bowl. Sprinkle over tortillas.
6. Bake for 5 to 7 minutes or until lightly browned.
7. Carefully cut each tortilla into quarters. Place one kiwi slice and two strawberry halves on top of each quarter.

Lemon Nachos

3	egg yolks	6	flour tortillas (each 6 inches)
¼ cup	plus 2 tsp white sugar	2 tsp	cinnamon
¼ cup	lemon juice (about 1 lemon)		

1. In a medium saucepan, heat egg yolks, ¼ cup of the sugar and lemon juice over low heat. Stir constantly with a wire whisk until mixture starts to thicken, making sure it doesn't boil.
2. Transfer to bowl. Place plastic wrap directly on the surface of the lemon mixture and refrigerate for at least an hour.
3. Place tortillas on cookie sheets that have been sprayed with cooking spray.
4. Preheat over to 400°F.
5. Mix remaining 2 tsp sugar and cinnamon in a small bowl. Sprinkle over tortillas.
6. Bake for 5 to 7 minutes or until lightly browned.
7. Carefully cut tortillas into quarters. Place a dollop of lemon mixture on each slice.

Sweet Strudels

The strudel is actually first cousin to the Chelsea bun. This recipe makes two strudels, each of which yields 10 to 12 slices.

1	recipe Chelsea Dough (p. 8)

Cheese and Raisin Filling

1 cup	partly skimmed ricotta cheese
2	egg whites, lightly beaten
1 tbsp	brown sugar
1 tbsp	fat-free plain yogurt
½ tsp	ground cinnamon
½ tsp	vanilla
½ tsp	lemon juice
¼ cup	raisins

Apple Filling

4	medium apples, peeled, cored and thinly sliced
¼	cup brown sugar
¼	cup white sugar
1 tsp	ground cinnamon
½ tsp	lemon juice
1 tbsp	low-fat margarine

Glaze

1	egg white
1 tsp	1% or 2% milk

1. To make Cheese and Raisin Filling, in a medium bowl, mix together cheese, egg whites, brown sugar, yogurt, cinnamon, vanilla and lemon juice with a fork. Stir in raisins.
2. To make Apple Filling, in a medium bowl, mix together apples, brown and white sugars, cinnamon and lemon juice.
3. In a large skillet, heat margarine over medium heat. Add apple mixture and cook for 2 to 3 minutes or until apples are soft.
4. On a floured surface, roll half the dough into a 9- x 12-inch rectangle.
5. Spread Cheese and Raisin Filling over the dough. Roll up jelly-roll style and pinch edge to seal.
6. Place widthwise across a cookie sheet that has been sprayed with cooking spray.
7. Repeat procedure with remaining dough and the Apple Filling. Place second roll on cookie sheet, leaving 3 inches between rolls.
8. Cover rolls with a tea towel and let rise for about 1 hour.
9. Preheat oven to 375°F.
10. Cut small steam vents across the top of each roll.
11. Mix together egg white and milk to make glaze.
12. Brush glaze over top of each roll. Bake for 25 minutes or until golden.
13. Slice each roll into 10 to 12 pieces.

Scones

These cakes, served in triangular wedges, originated in Scotland in the sixteenth century. The best part about making them is that they can be shaped simply by hand. This recipe makes 8 scones.

Blueberry Buttermilk Scones

2 cups	all-purpose flour	1 tsp	baking soda
1 cup	buttermilk	1 tsp	vanilla
¼ cup	white sugar	½ tsp	salt
3 tbsp	low-fat margarine, melted	½ cup	fresh blueberries
1 tbsp	baking powder	1½ cups	icing sugar
		2–3 tbsp	water OR orange juice

1. Preheat oven to 375°F.
2. Place flour, buttermilk, sugar, margarine, baking powder, baking soda, vanilla and salt in a large mixing bowl. Stir with a fork until just blended. Fold in blueberries.
3. Knead dough six or seven times on a surface that has been dusted with flour.
4. Pat the dough into a circle on a cookie sheet that has been sprayed with cooking spray. The circle should be about 9 inches in diameter, and the dough should be about ½ inch thick. With a serrated knife, cut circle into eight wedges.
5. Bake for 20 minutes or until dough looks like a large, hard cookie. Cool and recut, if necessary.
6. Mix icing sugar and water together with a fork. Drizzle over the individual wedges.

Chocolate Peanut Butter Scones

I knew my favourite flavour combination would turn up somewhere. This recipe makes 8 scones.

2 cups	all-purpose flour	¾ cup	calorie-reduced smooth peanut butter
½ cup	brown sugar	¼ cup	1% or 2% milk
1 tbsp	baking powder	2	eggs
1 tsp	baking soda	2 tsp	vanilla
½ tsp	salt	¾ cup	semi-sweet chocolate chips
¼ cup	cold stick-type low-fat margarine		

1. Preheat oven to 375°F.
2. Place flour, sugar, baking powder, baking soda and salt in a large mixing bowl. Stir with a wooden spoon until blended.
3. With two knives, a pastry cutter or your fingers, work in margarine until mixture resembles coarse oatmeal. Set aside.
4. In a small mixing bowl, stir together peanut butter, milk, eggs and vanilla. Add to flour mixture and mix well. Fold in chocolate chips.
5. Pat the dough into a circle on a cookie sheet that has been sprayed with cooking spray. The circle should be about 9 inches in diameter, and the dough should be about ½ inch thick. With a serrated knife, cut circle into eight wedges.
6. Bake for 20 minutes or until dough looks like a large, hard cookie. Cool and recut, if necessary.

Chocolate Madeleines

Madeleines are cookies that are baked in special pans that have sea-shell–shaped indentations. They are named after the pastry chef Madeleine Palmier, who resided in Commercy, France, in the nineteenth century. This recipe makes 24 cookies.

1 cup	sliced drained canned pears (packed in juice)	1 tsp	baking powder
		½ tsp	baking soda
1 tbsp	canola oil	4	egg whites
1 cup	all-purpose flour	½ cup	white sugar
3 tbsp	unsweetened cocoa	1 tsp	vanilla

1. Preheat oven to 375°F.
2. Place pears and oil in a blender and process until puréed, about 30 seconds.
3. In a small bowl, mix together flour, cocoa, baking powder and baking soda.
4. In a large mixing bowl, place egg whites and sugar. Using an electric mixer, beat at high speed for 5 minutes.
5. Add vanilla and beat for another 30 seconds.
6. With mixer at low speed, add dry ingredients alternately with pear purée, making three additions of dry ingredients and two of pear purée, and beating for 20 seconds after each addition.
7. Spoon about 1 tbsp batter in each shell shape in a madeleine pan that has been sprayed with cooking spray.
8. Bake for 15 minutes or until golden.

Herbal Teas

Many plants and herbs can be infused into teas with medicinal effects. Some popular herbal teas include –

Camomile tea – Infused with the flowers of the camomile plant, this tea is used as a gentle sedative and an aid in digestion.

Dandelion tea – Infused with dandelion root, which contains iron and calcium, this tea is used as a laxative and a digestive aid.

Fennel tea – Infused with fennel seeds, this tea has a licorice flavour. It is used as an aid in digestion and as an appetite suppressant.

Ginseng tea – Infused with ginseng root, this tea is used as a cold and cough remedy.

Peppermint tea – Infused with peppermint leaves, this tea is used to suppress nervous tension.

Sasparilla tea – Infused with the sasparilla root, this tea is known to be helpful in reducing arthritis symptoms.

Snowballs

You won't find any fat in these little gems. Throw ⅓ cup chocolate chips or crushed candy canes into the batter before baking for an extra little kick. This recipe yields between 12 and 24 Snowballs.

3	egg whites
½ tsp	cream of tartar
½ cup	white sugar
1 tsp	vanilla

1. Preheat oven to 300°F.
2. Place egg whites and cream of tartar in a medium mixing bowl. Using an electric mixer, beat at high speed until egg whites are foamy.
3. With mixer on, gradually add sugar in 1-tbsp increments until stiff peaks form. This should take 3 to 4 minutes. Add vanilla and continue beating for 1 more minute.
4. Drop cookies by rounded teaspoonfuls onto a cookie sheet that has been lined with foil and then sprayed with cooking spray.
5. Bake for 30 minutes or until lightly browned. Transfer to wire rack to cool completely.

Cranberry Lemon Biscotti

These crispy, twice-baked items are always favourites. This recipe makes about 12 cookies.

½ cup	dried cranberries	¼ tsp	baking soda
¼ cup	crème de cassis OR water	⅛ tsp	salt
½ cup	whole almonds	2	egg whites
1½ cups	all-purpose flour	¼ cup	canola oil
¼ cup	brown sugar	1 tsp	lemon extract
2 tbsp	white sugar	1 tsp	grated lemon zest
½ tsp	ground cinnamon		

1. In a medium bowl, soak cranberries in crème de cassis for 1 hour. Drain and set aside. Preheat oven to 375°F.
2. Toast almonds in a single layer for 10 minutes or until golden. Coarsely chop with a knife. Set aside.
3. In a large mixing bowl, whisk together flour, brown and white sugars, cinnamon, baking soda and salt.
4. Place egg whites, oil and lemon extract in a large mixing bowl. Using an electric mixer, beat at medium speed for 1 to 2 minutes.
5. With a wooden spoon, fold in flour mixture.
6. Add cranberries, almonds and lemon zest to batter and mix thoroughly. The dough should be sticky.
7. Place dough on a surface that has been dusted with flour. Using your hands, shape dough into a log about 12 inches long and 2½ to 3 inches long.
8. Line a cookie sheet with foil, shiny side up. Spray with cooking spray. Transfer log to the cookie sheet. Bake for 20 to 25 minutes or until lightly browned.
9. Transfer log to a cutting board and cut into 1-inch slices. Place slices cut side down on the cookie sheet. Bake for another 6 minutes. Flip slices over and bake for another 6 minutes or until lightly browned on top.

Little Lime Cheesecakes

This recipe should yield about 24 pieces.

Crust

1 cup	graham cracker crumbs
½ cup	crushed chocolate wafers
¼ cup	prune baby food
2 tbsp	white sugar

Filling

1 cup	low-fat cream cheese
1 can	(14 oz) low-fat sweetened condensed milk
6 tbsp	lime juice
2	egg yolks
1 tsp	vanilla
2	egg whites

¼ tsp	cream of tartar

Little Date Bites

Take a low-fat shortcut by substituting applesauce or other puréed fruit such as pears, bananas, peaches or prunes for most of the butter or shortening in any cake, muffin or bar recipe. This recipe makes 24 bites.

2½ cups	whole-wheat flour
¾ cup	brown sugar
1 tbsp	baking powder
¼ tsp	salt
1¼ cups	applesauce
2	egg whites
2 tbsp	low-fat margarine, melted
1 tsp	vanilla
½ cup	chopped dates
¼ cup	raisins
¼ cup	chopped pecans

1. Preheat oven to 400°F.
2. In a medium bowl, mix together flour, brown sugar, baking powder and salt with a wooden spoon.
3. In a large mixing bowl, place applesauce, egg whites, margarine and vanilla. Using an electric mixer, beat at medium speed for 20 seconds.
4. Add flour mixture to wet ingredients with a wooden spoon and mix until just blended. Add dates, raisins and pecans.
5. Spoon batter into the cups of a mini muffin pan that has been sprayed with cooking spray.
6. Bake for 18 minutes or until lightly browned.

Double Berry Muffin Tops

One way to reduce the fat content of your baked goods is to use buttermilk, which is low in fat, as the main liquid ingredient. This recipe yields 12 muffin tops.

1 cup	all-purpose flour	1 tsp	vanilla
½ cup	white sugar	1 cup	quick-cooking rolled oats
1 tbsp	baking powder	½ cup	fresh blueberries
¼ tsp	salt	½ cup	fresh raspberries
1 cup	buttermilk	1 tsp	grated orange rind
3	egg whites		
2 tbsp	canola oil		

1. Preheat oven to 400°F.
2. In a medium bowl, mix together flour, sugar, baking powder and salt with a wooden spoon.
3. In a large mixing bowl, place buttermilk, egg whites, oil and vanilla. Using an electric mixer, beat at medium speed for 20 seconds.
4. Reduce speed to low and add rolled oats. Beat until blended, about 15 seconds.
5. With a wooden spoon, add flour mixture. Stir until blended. Add blueberries, raspberries and orange rind and stir well.
6. Spoon batter into muffin top tins that have been sprayed with cooking spray.
7. Bake for 18 minutes or until slightly browned on top.

The Tea Treasure Chest

Tea was first introduced to Europe in the mid-sixteenth century by Portuguese explorers who had encountered it in China. Dutch voyagers brought it back from the Far East. By the nineteenth century, it had become Britain's national beverage.

Most tea is grown in China, Japan, Indonesia, India or Sri Lanka. There are three main types of teas: black tea, which is produced by drying and fermenting tea leaves; green tea, which is produced by steaming the leaves; and oolong tea, which is produced by partially fermenting and partially steaming the leaves.

SOME POPULAR BLACK TEAS INCLUDE –

Earl Grey – This tea is infused with the oil of bergamot. It is the traditional afternoon tea of the Queen.

English breakfast – This tea goes particularly well with milk and sugar. It is a blend of two black teas – Assam, which has a malty taste, and Keenum, which has a fruity, sweet aroma.

Irish breakfast – Stronger than English Breakfast, this tea is a blend of Assam and Ceylon teas. Use milk and sugar moderately.

Lapsang Souchong – This tea is a variety of Chinese black tea; it has a smoky flavour.

Orange pekoe – From India and Sri Lanka, this tea is made from young leaves and leaf buds.

SOME VARIETIES OF GREEN TEA INCLUDE –

Sencha – a Japanese tea with a delicate flavour

Young Hyson – a full-flavoured tea made from the first leaves of the season

Jasmine flower – a green tea scented with jasmine flowers

Double mint – a green tea scented with peppermint and spearmint

SOME VARIETIES OF OOLONG TEA INCLUDE –

Oolong choice – golden in colour and fruity in taste

Oolong fancy – flavoured with apricot

Coffee – Your Best Friend

When was the last time you missed your morning coffee? If this question stumps you, then you will realize what a strong bond you have with your morning brew.

The practice of infusing ground roasted coffee beans in water began in Arabia in the fifteenth century. By the seventeenth century, the British had opened up coffee houses. In the United States, coffee drinking grew in popularity when the tax imposed on tea led to the Boston Tea Party.

Coffee beans come from different parts of the world –

From the Americas

Columbia – Coffee has a rich aroma and slightly nutty flavour.
Costa Rica – Coffee has a medium body and a slightly chocolatey flavour.
Hawaii – Coffee has a medium body; most of the beans are from Kona.
Guatemala – Coffee has a full body and a slightly smoky flavour.
Mexico – Coffee has a delicate, sweet flavour.

From Indonesia

Java – Coffee is full bodied with an intense chocolatey flavour; beans resemble the cocoa pod.
Sumatra – Coffee is heavy bodied and syrupy, with a slightly chocolatey flavour.

From Africa

Ethiopia – Coffee is very rare and has a strong flavour.
Kenya – Coffee is full bodied and has an intense flavour.

A Variety of Coffee Beverages

Espresso is made by forcing steam at high pressure through finely ground beans. It is served without milk or cream.
Cappuccino is nicknamed "frothy coffee." This drink, Italian in origin, is made up of three parts – one-third espresso, one-third steamed milk, one-third milk froth.
Caffe latte is made with steamed milk and one or two shots of espresso.
Café au lait is like caffe latte but is made with brewed coffee instead of espresso.
Café mocha is made with hot chocolate, whipped cream and one or two shots of espresso.
Mochaccino is made with hot chocolate, milk froth and one or two shots of espresso.
Macchiato is made with milk froth and one or two shots of espresso.

APRÈS-SKI

From all my years of skiing, I am certain of one thing: après-ski snacks must be as substantial as dinner. There is no way that you can bring cold, tired skiers off the hill and offer them a party sandwich. They'll just stay until you bring out the real stuff anyways. So why not go for broke at 5 p.m.?

Tell your guests to bring a change of clothes with them so that they don't have to sit around in their ski suits and long underwear. Ignore all pleas to take showers.

These recipes were written to feed a crowd of 12, but do not fret if a few stray snowmobilers drop by.

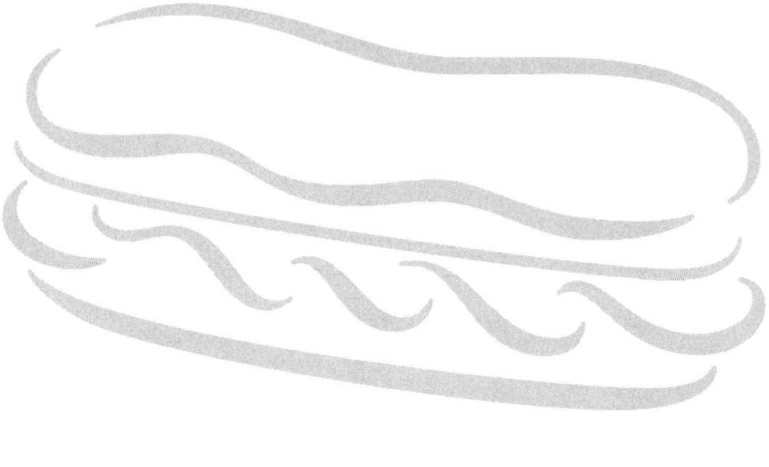

Menu

Serves 12

Corn and Black Bean Salad

A Batch of Biscuits

A Hero's Welcome

Shepherd's Chicken Pot Pie

Mac 'n' Cheese

Roulade of Veal

Risotto on Its Own

Crêpe It Yourself

Crêpe Toppers:

- *Suzette Sauce*
- *Strawberry Sauce*
- *Pineapple Sauce*

Presentation

Your presentation should reflect a casual ease. Since an après-ski usually takes place at a vacation residence, a lot of the items have to be transported from home.

The Mac 'n' Cheese and the Shepherd's Chicken Pot Pie are served in whatever they were cooked in. Glass baking dishes can be fitted into handy wicker containers for serving. Make sure you have the appropriate serving pieces and trivets on the table.

Large platters can be used for the Corn and Black Bean Salad, the risotto and the Veal Roulade. If you have time, line these platters with curly endive leaves.

Serve the biscuits in a large wicker basket lined with a colourful cloth napkin. Put the Hero's Welcome sandwiches out on a cutting board and allow guests to cut their own slices.

The crêpes will be served after the meal is completed and the table is cleared off. You will need one or two of your guests in the kitchen to make the crêpes. Your guests will go into the kitchen to get their crêpes and toppings. You will supervise from your seat by the fire.

A large tray filled with pistachio nuts, sugar-coated peanuts, chocolate-covered raisins, cashews almonds, jujubes and other assorted candies would make an easy and useful centrepiece. For something more whimsical, you could take a child's ski boot, clean it up and use it as a vase for pussywillows. As a final touch, take six large apples and make them into candle holders by taking a small knife and making a hole in the top of each apple a bit larger than a tea light. Insert tea lights into apples. Surround the centrepiece with them.

For the musical accompaniment, I once again enter nostalgia mode and choose old familiar favourites: *The Stranger* by Billy Joel, the Eagles' *Greatest Hits* and *The Heart of Chicago* by Chicago.

Preparation Schedule

Although I am not a big fan of freezing cooked food, in this situation the convenience greatly outweighs any disadvantages.

Up to Two Weeks Before

The Mac 'n' Cheese is a good candidate for freezing. It can be made up to two weeks in advance, whenever spare time crops up. Cook it thoroughly. Cover with foil. Place the covered casserole dish in a plastic bag. Secure with a twist tie. Freeze.

The Day Before

1. Make Corn and Black Bean Salad. Store in an airtight container in the refrigerator.
2. Make Strawberry Sauce and Pineapple Sauce. Store in airtight containers in the refrigerator.
3. Make hero sandwiches and refrigerate.
4. Take the casserole out of the freezer and place it in the refrigerator overnight to thaw.

That Day

1. Preheat oven to 350°F.
2. Prepare Veal Roulade and bake for 1 hour.
3. Prepare the Shepherd's Chicken Pot Pie and set aside.
4. Prepare biscuits and set aside.
5. Take roulade out of the oven. Increase heat to 400°F.
6. Bake pot pie for 30 minutes.
7. While pot pie is baking, cut up roulade and place on serving platter. Assemble ingredients for the risotto.
8. Take pot pie out of the oven. Increase heat to 425°F. Bake biscuits for 15 minutes.
9. Take biscuits out of the oven. Lower heat to 350°F. Bake Mac 'n' Cheese and hero sandwiches for 15 to 20 minutes or until heated through.
10. Meanwhile, make risotto.

11. After Mac 'n' Cheese and the sandwiches are heated, turn off the oven, cover them and leave them in there until the risotto is done.
12. When risotto is done, remove to serving platter. Take Mac 'n' Cheese and sandwiches out of the oven.
13. After dinner, prepare the crêpe batter. Take the Strawberry and Pineapple Sauces out of the refrigerator and place in bowls.
14. Prepare Suzette Sauce and keep on simmer while crêpes are being made. Serve it right from the saucepan.

Corn and Black Bean Salad

Black beans, which are oval shaped and nutty in flavour, are a good source of fibre and protein. This recipe serves 12.

3 cups	cooked corn (from about 6 ears)	1 tbsp	minced seeded jalapeño pepper
2 cans	(each 14 oz) black beans, drained (or about ½ lb dried – see note)	½ cup	lime juice (3 to 4 limes)
		¼ cup	minced fresh parsley
		2 tbsp	minced fresh garlic
4	plum tomatoes, cut in ¼-inch cubes	1 tsp	ground cumin
		¾ cup	olive oil
1	medium red pepper, cored, seeded and cut in ¼-inch cubes	½ cup	minced fresh cilantro
		3 tbsp	freshly grated Parmesan cheese
½	purple onion, cut in ¼ inch cubes		

1. In a large mixing bowl, mix together corn, beans, tomatoes, red pepper, onion and jalapeño pepper.
2. Place lime juice, parsley, garlic and cumin in the work bowl of a food processor. Blend for 10 seconds. With machine running, pour in oil and blend for 20 more seconds.
3. Pour dressing over corn mixture and blend thoroughly. Sprinkle cilantro and Parmesan cheese over top.

Note: If you are using dried beans, soak them overnight and then discard the water. To cook, simmer beans in three parts water to one part beans for 1 hour.

A Batch of Biscuits

Hot from the oven, these will disappear in a flash. This recipe yields about 12 biscuits.

1½ cups	all-purpose flour
1 cup	cake and pastry flour
2 tbsp	baking powder
2 tbsp	white sugar
½ tsp	salt
⅓ cup	cold shortening, stick-type low-fat margarine OR butter
¼ cup	shredded low-fat cheddar cheese
1 cup	buttermilk
3 tbsp	low-fat margarine, melted

1. Preheat oven to 425°F.
2. In a large mixing bowl, blend together flours, baking powder, sugar and salt with a wooden spoon until thoroughly blended.
3. Using two knives, a pastry cutter or your hands, work shortening into the dry ingredients until mixture resembles coarse oatmeal. Stir in cheese.
4. Make a well in the centre of the mixture. Add buttermilk and stir until dough forms a ball.
5. Place the dough on a surface that has been dusted with flour. Dust your hands with flour and knead the dough for 1 minute.
6. Press the dough into a 1-inch-thick round. Dip a 2-inch round cookie cutter in flour and cut out biscuits. Reroll the scraps to use up all the dough.
7. Dip each biscuit into margarine and place on a cookie sheet that has been sprayed with cooking spray.
8. Bake for 15 minutes or until lightly browned.

Hearty Soups

Hearty soups can certainly take the chill out of the air. Warm up with Minestrone or Mushroom and Barley Soup, each of which provides 12 servings, or Salmon Corn Chowder, which yields 8 portions.

Minestrone

2 tbsp	olive oil
1 cup	thinly shredded green cabbage
2	medium leeks (white part and 1 inch green part), quartered lengthwise and thinly sliced
2	medium carrots, sliced into ¼-inch rounds
1	shallot, finely chopped
1 tbsp	minced fresh garlic
6–7 cups	vegetable or low-fat chicken or beef broth
1 can	(28 oz) diced plum tomatoes, undrained
4	small new potatoes cut in quarters
2 tbsp	minced fresh basil
1 tbsp	minced fresh oregano
1 can	(14 oz) red kidney beans, drained
½ cup	small pasta (orzo or tubettini)
2 tbsp	freshly grated Parmesan cheese
2 tbsp	minced fresh parsley
Salt and pepper	

1. In a large soup pot, heat oil over medium heat. Sauté cabbage, leeks, carrots, shallot and garlic for 5 to 7 minutes or until wilted and golden.
2. Add broth and tomatoes to soup pot and bring to a boil. Add potatoes, basil and oregano. Reduce heat to simmer and cover. Cook for 1 to 1½ hours.
3. Add kidney beans and pasta and cook, covered, for an additional 10 minutes or until pasta is al dente.
4. Stir in cheese and parsley. Add salt and pepper to taste.

Mushroom and Barley Soup

1 oz	dried porcini or shiitake mushrooms	2	shallots finely chopped
1 cup	boiling water	1 tbsp	minced fresh garlic
2 tbsp	low-fat margarine	1 tbsp	soy sauce
2 cups	thinly sliced button mushrooms	1 tbsp	all-purpose flour
2	medium carrots, sliced in ¼-inch rounds	7–8 cups	low-fat beef broth
2	medium onions, cut in ½-inch cubes	1 cup	pearl barley
2	stalks celery, thinly sliced	½ tsp	salt
		½ tsp	dried rosemary
		2 tbsp	minced fresh parsley

1. In a small bowl, soak mushrooms in boiling water for 30 minutes. Drain, reserving liquid, and coarsely chop mushrooms.
2. In a large soup pot, heat margarine over medium heat. Add button mushrooms, carrots, onions, celery, shallots and garlic and sauté for 5 to 7 minutes or until wilted and golden. Stir in soy sauce.
3. Reduce heat to low. Sprinkle flour over vegies and stir until blended.
4. Combine broth with reserved mushroom liquid and add to soup pot, a little at a time, stirring constantly. Increase heat to medium high and bring soup to a boil. Add barley, salt and rosemary.
5. Reduce heat to low and cover. Cook for 1 hour. Ladle soup into bowls and sprinkle with parsley.

Salmon Corn Chowder

2 tbsp	low-fat margarine	5–6 cups	vegetable or low-fat chicken broth
1	large onion, cut in ½ inch cubes	5	small new potatoes, peeled and quartered
1	medium carrot, cut in ¼-inch rounds	3 cups	cooked corn
1	stalk celery, thinly sliced	1 cup	2% milk
1 tsp	minced fresh garlic	1 can	(7 oz) boneless salmon, drained and separated into chunks
2 tbsp	all-purpose flour		
¼ tsp	cayenne	1 tsp	paprika

1. In a large soup pot, heat margarine over medium heat. Sauté onion, carrot, celery and garlic for 5 to 7 minutes or until wilted and golden.
2. Reduce heat to low. Sprinkle flour and cayenne over vegies and stir until thoroughly blended.
3. Add broth to soup pot a little at a time, stirring constantly, and then bring to a boil. Add potatoes and 1 cup of the corn. Cover and let simmer for 20 minutes or until potatoes are tender.
4. In food processor, process soup in batches for 15 seconds or until puréed. Return soup to the pot.
5. Whisk in milk over medium-low heat. Add remaining 2 cups corn, salmon and paprika.

A Hero's Welcome

Cut these hero sandwiches into individual slices and serve them to your guests as appetizers. Each loaf yields 6 to 8 slices.

3 cups	sliced zucchini
4	large tomatoes, cut in ½-inch slices
3	large portobello mushrooms, cut in ½-inch slices and stems removed
2	large purple onions, cut in ½-inch slices
2 tbsp	olive oil
1 tsp	salt
½ tsp	pepper
2	sprigs fresh basil
2	sprigs fresh rosemary
1	bunch spinach, stems removed
1 tsp	low-fat margarine
4 tsp	minced fresh garlic
1 tsp	white sugar
2	loaves (each 1 lb) French bread
½ cup	fat-free mayonnaise
¼ cup	chopped green olives
1 tbsp	Dijon mustard
½	cup goat cheese

1. Preheat oven to 450°F.
2. Place zucchini, tomatoes, mushrooms and onions in a roasting pan that has been sprayed with cooking spray. Drizzle olive oil over top. Sprinkle with salt and pepper.
3. Place basil and rosemary sprigs over top of vegetables. Bake for 20 minutes or until onions are tender.
4. While vegetables are cooking, place spinach in a vegetable steamer and cook until wilted, about 5 minutes. Rinse under cold water. Squeeze dry and coarsely chop.
5. In a medium skillet, heat margarine over medium-low heat. Sauté spinach and 1 tbsp of the garlic for 2 minutes. Sprinkle with sugar. Set aside.
6. Cut loaves in half lengthwise. Scoop out the insides leaving ½ to 1 inch of bread near the crust.
7. Remove vegetables from the oven. Discard basil and rosemary sprigs.
8. Place mayonnaise, olives, mustard and remaining 1 tsp garlic in a small mixing bowl. Whisk together until blended.
9. Spread tops and bottoms of loaves with equal amounts of mayonnaise mixture.
10. Line the two bottoms of the loaves with equal amounts of zucchini mixture.

11. Spread spinach mixture over the zucchini mixture.
12. Sprinkle half of the goat cheese over top of each sandwich.
13. Place tops of loaves on sandwiches. Wrap tightly in foil and refrigerate for a couple of hours or overnight.
14. Before serving, warm wrapped sandwiches in preheated 350°F oven for 15 minutes. Cut each loaf into six to eight slices.

Shepherd's Chicken Pot Pie

Take the mashed potato topping from shepherd's pie and the chicken and vegetable filling from chicken pot pie, and you've created this hybrid. If you don't have any leftover chicken or turkey in your refrigerator, you can always cook a whole chicken breast, an onion and a carrot in 3 cups low-fat chicken broth for 45 minutes or until cooked through. Or just do what I do and purchase a barbecue chicken from the grocery store. This pie will serve 8 to 12 small portions.

6–8 cups	water	¼ cup	fat-free plain yogurt
8	medium potatoes, unpeeled, quartered	1 tsp	Dijon mustard
2 tsp	canola oil	1 tbsp	minced fresh thyme
1 cup	cubed onions	1 tbsp	minced fresh parsley
1 cup	snow peas	3 cups	cubed cooked chicken
1 cup	sliced button mushrooms	1 cup	frozen peas, thawed
2	large carrots, cut in matchsticks	4 tbsp	low-fat margarine, melted
3 tbsp	low-fat margarine	1 tsp	salt
3 tbsp	instant blending flour	½ tsp	pepper
2 cups	low-fat chicken broth	2 tbsp	freshly grated Parmesan cheese

1. In a large saucepan, bring water to a boil over high heat. Add potatoes. Reduce heat to medium low. Cover and cook for 20 minutes.
2. Meanwhile, in a large skillet, heat oil over medium heat. Sauté onions, snow peas, mushrooms and carrots for 3 to 4 minutes or until softened. Remove to a large plate.
3. In same skillet, heat margarine over medium-low heat. Whisk in flour. Gradually pour in chicken broth, whisking until well blended.
4. Whisk in yogurt and mustard and blend thoroughly. Mix in thyme and parsley.
5. Add chicken and peas to the skillet and stir well. Transfer the mixture to an ungreased 3-quart casserole dish. Add onion mixture and blend thoroughly.
6. By this time, the potatoes should be fork tender. Drain and rinse with cold water. Peel skins.
7. Preheat oven to 400°F.

8. Pass potato pieces through a potato ricer into a large mixing bowl. With a wooden spoon, add melted margarine, salt and pepper, and stir until smooth and blended.
9. Top chicken mixture with mashed potatoes. Sprinkle with Parmesan cheese. Bake, uncovered, for 30 minutes or until lightly browned.

Mac 'n' Cheese

Forever the favourite comfort food, this dish evokes pleasant childhood memories. This recipe makes between 8 and 12 portions.

8 cups	water
4 cups	elbow macaroni
½ cup	all-purpose flour
½ tsp	dry mustard
3½ cups	skim milk OR buttermilk
1 cup	shredded low-fat cheddar cheese
¾ cup	shredded low-fat mozzarella cheese
½ cup	low-fat cream cheese
¼ cup	freshly grated Parmesan cheese
1 tsp	pepper
½ tsp	salt
¼ cup	dry breadcrumbs
1 tbsp	low-fat margarine, melted

1. In a large saucepan, bring water to a boil.
2. Add the macaroni and boil until al dente, about 7 minutes.
3. Drain. Rinse under cold water, drain and set aside.
4. Preheat oven to 375°F.
5. In a large saucepan, whisk together flour and mustard. Gradually whisk in milk over low heat until well blended.
6. Add the four cheeses, stirring until thoroughly blended. Pour into 3-quart casserole dish that has been sprayed with cooking spray.
7. With a wooden spoon, stir in macaroni. Add pepper and salt.
8. In a small bowl, mix together breadcrumbs and margarine. Sprinkle over casserole. Bake, uncovered, for 25 minutes or until topping is golden.

Roulade of Veal

A roulade, which is part of French cuisine, is a dish that is rolled up. For variety, boneless chicken breasts, butterflied and pounded, may be substituted for the veal cutlets. Cut each roll into thirds to yield 12 portions.

4	veal cutlets (1 lb)	½ cup	goat cheese
5 tbsp	all-purpose flour	1 tbsp	minced fresh parsley
	Salt and pepper	1 tsp	minced fresh garlic
1	large chicken and veal sausage, casing removed (about ¼ lb)	1 tsp	olive oil
		3 tbsp	low-fat margarine
		2 cups	low-fat chicken broth

1. Dust cutlets with 2 tbsp of the flour and sprinkle with salt and pepper. Set aside.
2. In a medium nonstick skillet, crumble sausage and sauté for 2 to 3 minutes or until no longer pink. Set aside.
3. Spread goat cheese in equal portions on cutlets. Sprinkle sausage over the cheese.
4. In a small bowl, mix together parsley and garlic with a fork. Spoon on top of sausage layer.
5. Roll up each cutlet jelly-roll style and secure with toothpicks.
6. In a large skillet, heat oil over medium heat. Add veal rolls and sauté for 2 to 3 minutes or until evenly browned. Place on large dish and set aside.
7. In a small saucepan, heat margarine over medium-low heat. Reduce heat to low and gradually whisk in remaining 3 tbsp flour until mixture is well blended. Gradually pour in chicken stock, whisking until sauce is smooth and thick, 2 to 3 minutes.
8. Preheat oven to 350°F.
9. Place 3 tbsp of the broth mixture on the bottom of an ungreased 9- x 13-inch glass baking dish. Place rolls on top. Pour the rest of the broth mixture on top of the rolls.
10. Cover dish with foil and bake for 1 hour or until veal is fork tender.
11. To serve, remove toothpicks and carefully slice each roll into three pieces. Transfer to platter.

Stuffing Your Roulade in Other Ways

Each of these stuffings will fill 4 veal cutlets.

Breadcrumb Stuffing

- 2 tsp low-fat margarine
- 1 small bunch green onions (green parts removed), thinly sliced
- ½ cup thinly sliced celery
- ½ cup thinly sliced button mushrooms
- 1 tsp minced fresh garlic
- 1 tsp minced fresh parsley
- 1 cup dry breadcrumbs
- ½ cup vegetable or low-fat chicken broth

1. In a medium skillet, heat margarine over medium heat. Sauté onions, celery and mushrooms for 3 to 4 minutes or until softened. Add garlic and parsley.
2. Place mixture in large mixing bowl. With a wooden spoon, stir in breadcrumbs. Gradually add broth, stirring, until mixture holds together.

Bulgur Stuffing

¾ cup	boiling water (or enough to cover bulgur)	¼ cup	pine nuts
½ cup	bulgur	1 tbsp	minced fresh parsley
1 tsp	low-fat margarine	½ tsp	ground cumin
1	bunch green onions (green parts removed), thinly sliced	2 tbsp	vegetable or low-fat chicken broth

1. In a small bowl, pour boiling water over bulgur. Let soak for about 30 minutes or until most of the water is absorbed. Drain and set aside.
2. In a medium skillet, heat margarine over medium heat. Sauté green onions and pine nuts for 3 to 4 minutes or until golden. Add parsley and cumin and sauté for 2 more minutes.
3. Place mixture in a medium mixing bowl. With a wooden spoon, stir in the bulgur. Gradually add the broth, stirring, until the mixture holds together.

Rice Stuffing

1 cup	water	1	small bunch green onions (green parts removed), thinly sliced
½ cup	long-grain rice	1 tbsp	soy sauce
1 tsp	low-fat margarine		
1 tsp	olive oil		

1. In a medium saucepan, bring water to a boil. Add rice and margarine. Cover and reduce heat to simmer. Cook for about 25 minutes or until water is absorbed and rice is tender but firm.
2. In a large skillet, heat oil over medium heat. Add green onions and sauté for 3 to 4 minutes or until golden. With a wooden spoon, stir in rice and sauté for 2 minutes. Add soy sauce and sauté until rice is thoroughly coated.

Risotto on Its Own

Since this is the last item to be made before dinner I have decided to forgo any vegie, chicken or meat additions for the sake of ease and simplicity. This recipe yields 8 to 12 small portions.

7–8 cups	vegetable or low-fat chicken broth
2 tbsp	olive oil
1½ cups	cubed purple onion
1 tbsp	minced fresh garlic
3 cups	Arborio rice
1½ cups	dry white wine
2 cups	freshly grated Parmesan cheese
2 tbsp	minced fresh parsley
	Salt and pepper

1. In a medium saucepan, bring broth to a simmer over medium heat. Reduce heat to low and let stand until ready for use.
2. In a large skillet, heat oil over medium heat. Sauté onions and garlic for 2 to 3 minutes or until softened.
3. Add rice to skillet and cook, stirring, for 2 minutes or until the rice turns opaque.
4. Reduce heat to medium low. Add ½ cup of the wine to the skillet and stir until it is absorbed by the rice. Repeat this step twice.
5. Add 1 cup of the broth to the rice and stir until it is absorbed. Continue to add broth in ½-cup increments, allowing broth to be absorbed each time. Ultimately, the grains should be tender yet firm, and the mixture should be creamy.
6. Sprinkle cheese and parsley over top and stir until just blended. Add salt and pepper to taste. Serve immediately.

Crêpe It Yourself

Since dinner will be over early, there will still be a whole evening ahead of you. Dessert making becomes the evening's entertainment. This recipe yields 10 to 12 crêpes.

1½ cups	skim milk
4	eggs
1 cup	all-purpose flour
¼ cup	white sugar

1. In a large bowl, whisk milk and eggs together until blended.
2. In a small bowl, combine flour and sugar. Gradually whisk dry ingredients into egg mixture until thoroughly blended.
3. Coat a 7-inch crêpe skillet with cooking spray. Pour 2 tbsp batter into the pan and swirl the batter so that it evenly coats the pan. Over medium heat, cook for about 45 seconds on one side.
4. To turn crêpe over, lift an edge with a fork, grab it with your thumb and index finger and flip it over. Cook for another 30 seconds.
5. Slide crêpe onto a plate covered with a paper towel. Cover with another paper towel.
6. Stack crêpes on plate, using paper towel to separate them.

Crêpe Toppers

Fold the crêpe in half from right to left and then again from bottom to top. Then pour on the sauce. Or top crêpes with fresh berries, sliced bananas and icing sugar.

Suzette Sauce

This recipe yields ½ to 1 cup of sauce.

¼ cup	stick-type low-fat margarine
⅓ cup	icing sugar
2 tbsp	lemon or orange juice
2 tsp	lemon or orange rind
2 tbsp	cognac, bourbon OR rum

In a medium saucepan, heat margarine over medium heat. Whisk in sugar, lemon juice and lemon rind and stir until thoroughly blended. Add cognac and bring to a boil. Reduce heat to low and cook for another minute.

Strawberry Sauce

This recipe yields about two cups of sauce.

2 cups	fat-free plain yogurt
1 cup	sliced strawberries
1 /2 tsp	ground cinnamon

Mix all ingredients together in a small bowl.

Pineapple Sauce

This recipe yields about two cups of sauce.

2 cups	unsweetened crushed pineapple
1½ cups	fat-free pineapple yogurt
¼ cup	orange juice

Place all ingredients in the work bowl of a food processor. Blend for 20 seconds.

HAPPY BIRTHDAY, KIDDO!

Some of our best childhood memories are of birthday parties – being the centre of attention, collecting all those presents, enjoying the laughter, the commotion and the food.

This particular set of recipes will appeal not only to the children who attend the party, but also to their parents (a.k.a. kids at heart).

Menu

Serves 12

Child-Style Appetizers:

- *Tuna Bites*
- *Celery Crunches*
- *Nibbler's Mix*

Monte Cristo Sandwiches

Chicken Fingers and Dipping Sauces:

- *Sweet Mustard*
- *Plum Sauce*
- *Barbecue Sauce*

Fake Fries

Mini Burgers

Lemonade with Pint-Sized Fruit Kebabs

Black and White Sandwiches

The Birthday Cake

Presentation

Since this party is for children, a casual and fantasylike atmosphere should prevail. You will need strong, colourful paper plates and napkins of two sizes (dinner size and dessert size) and plastic forks and spoons.

Use a plastic pail (the kind the kids use at the beach) and some Frisbees as your serving bowls and plates. Also, gather together all the plastic tumblers and platters that you use outdoors in the summertime. They will also work well as serving dishes.

Arrange the Tuna Bites and Celery Crunches on Frisbees lined with curly endive lettuce. Use the plastic pail as a serving bowl for the Nibbler's Mix.

Place the Monte Cristo Sandwiches and the Mini Burgers on their own separate platters. Set out small bowls for ketchup, mustard and relish.

One large round platter can accommodate the Chicken Fingers and Fake Fries, arranged in a spokelike fashion. Set out small bowls for the three dipping sauces. You may want to put little place cards beside the bowls with the names of the sauces on them. Put out the pitcher of lemonade and tumblers with the kebabs.

The centrepiece for the table will be the candy-covered birthday cake. Surround it with jujubes, licorice, small chocolate bars and chocolate kisses.

Clear off the table for the lighting of the cake. Bring out the platters of Black and White Sandwiches.

The perfect musical accompaniment would be *Songs in the Key of Springfield* by The Simpsons and the soundtracks to *Space Jam* and *The Lion King*.

Preparation Schedule

Plain cakes freeze beautifully, allowing the cook some leeway in preparation time.

Up to Two Weeks Before

1. Bake the four 9-inch cakes. Take them out of their pans, wrap individually in foil and freeze.
2. Make paper stencils for the birthday cake.

The Day Before

1. Make the three dipping sauces. Store in airtight containers in the refrigerator.
2. Make the crumb mixture for the Chicken Fingers. Store in a resealable plastic bag.
3. Make the Nibbler's Mix. Store in resealable plastic bags.
4. Make the lemonade. Transfer to a covered pitcher and chill.
5. Take cakes out of the freezer.
6. Make Black and White Sandwiches and put in the freezer.

That Day

1. Make the Tuna Bites and the Celery Crunches.
2. Make the Pint-Sized Kebabs.
3. Make icing. Set up and decorate birthday cake.
4. Assemble Chicken Fingers.
5. Preheat oven to 400°F.
6. Bake Chicken Fingers for 10 minutes. Turn over and bake for 7 more minutes.
7. While they are baking, cut up and season the Fake Fries.
8. Take Chicken Fingers out of the oven and transfer to a foil container. Cover with foil.
9. Place Fake Fries in the oven. Bake for about 20 minutes. Turn over and bake for another 10 to 15 minutes.
10. Meanwhile, make patties for Mini Burgers and transfer to a foil container. Cover with foil.

11. Assemble Monte Cristo Sandwiches and dip in egg mixture. Transfer to a large platter and set aside.
12. Take fries out of the oven and transfer to a foil container. Cover with foil. Turn heat to broil.
13. Cook burgers for 5 minutes per side. While they are in the oven, cook Monte Cristo Sandwiches.
14. Turn off oven. Place foil containers in the oven to keep warm.
15. Put out the dipping sauces, condiments, lemonade, appetizers and Nibbler's Mix. Remove everything from the oven and place on the table.

Child-Style Appetizers

Kids are people too. It's just that their tastes are a little less sophisticated. At times adults prefer a little less sophistication too.

Tuna Bites

Makes 16.

2 cans	(each 7 oz) water-packed tuna, drained	1 tsp	lemon juice
1/3 cup	fat-free mayonnaise	1/4 tsp	salt
2 tbsp	pickle relish	4	English muffins, halved

1. Place tuna, mayonnaise, relish, lemon juice and salt in the work bowl of a food processor and process for 10 seconds or until blended OR use a large mixing bowl and blend with a fork.
2. Place English muffin halves on a work surface. Spread tuna mixture on each half. Cut each piece in half and transfer to a serving platter.

Celery Crunches

Makes 32.

8	celery stalks	1/4 cup	peanut butter
1/4 cup	low-fat cream cheese		

Place stalks on work surface. Spread cream cheese on four stalks and peanut butter on four stalks. Cut each stalk in quarters and transfer to a serving platter.

Nibbler's Mix

Even with tons of food, it wouldn't be a party without a bowl of munchies. This mixture yields enough for at least 12 munchers.

1 tbsp	low-fat margarine	1½ cups	raisins
1½ cups	salted shelled peanuts	1 cup	shredded coconut
½ cup	sunflower seeds, shelled	½ cup	dried banana chips
4 cups	popcorn	½ cup	chopped dried apricots

1. In a large skillet, heat margarine over medium heat. Sauté peanuts and sunflower seeds until browned, about 2 to 3 minutes. Transfer to serving bowl.
2. Add popcorn, raisins, coconut, banana chips and apricots to the bowl and mix thoroughly.

Loot Bag Goodies

Every birthday party guest deserves a little present of their own.

Candy Apples

This recipe makes 12 apples.

2 cups	white sugar	½ tsp	red food colouring
1¾ cups	light corn syrup	½ cup	sliced almonds
1 cup	water	12	medium apples, stems removed
¼ tsp	cream of tartar		
1 tsp	lemon juice	12	wooden Popsicle sticks

1. In a large saucepan, heat sugar, corn syrup, water and cream of tartar over medium-high heat. Stir constantly with a wire whisk until sugar is dissolved and mixture boils. Cook until temperature on candy thermometer reaches 250°F.
2. Remove from heat and stir in lemon juice and food colouring. Place the saucepan in a larger pan of warm water so that the sugar mixture does not stiffen while you prepare the apples.
3. Place almonds in a single layer on a plate.
4. Press a stick into stem end of each apple. Dip each apple into the syrup and twirl to coat. Dip lightly into nuts.
5. Place apples on a cookie sheet that has been lined with wax paper and then sprayed with cooking spray. Allow to harden, about 2 to 3 hours.

Monte Cristo Sandwiches

The Monte Cristo sandwich is a grilled cheese that has been "French toasted." This recipe yields 16 small sandwiches.

1	bunch broccoli, cut into florets	4	slices cheddar cheese (each 1 oz)
8	slices whole-wheat bread	6	eggs
		2 tsp	skim milk
		2 tsp	butter OR margarine

1. In a vegetable steamer, cook broccoli until tender yet firm, about 8 minutes. Chop into small pieces.
2. Put four slices of the bread on a work surface. Place one piece of the cheese on top of each slice. Place equal portions of broccoli on top of cheese slices. Top with remaining four bread slices.
3. Place eggs and milk in a large mixing bowl. Beat with a fork for 20 seconds. Carefully immerse each sandwich in egg mixture, making sure that any excess drips off. Place sandwiches on a large plate.
4. In a large skillet, heat 1 tsp of the butter over medium heat. Place two of the sandwiches in the pan and cook for 2 to 3 minutes or until browned. Flip over and cook for an additional 2 minutes. Transfer to serving platter. Repeat with remaining 1 tsp of butter and last two sandwiches. Cut each sandwich in quarters.

Chicken Fingers

These appetizers are a guaranteed crowd pleaser. This recipe makes 16 fingers.

4	boneless skinless chicken breasts (1–½ lb)	½ tsp	minced fresh garlic
	Salt, pepper and paprika	2 cups	dry breadcrumbs
2 tbsp	all-purpose flour	2 cups	cornflake crumbs
2	eggs, beaten	2 tbsp	sesame seeds
		1 tbsp	freshly grated Parmesan cheese

1. Preheat oven to 400°F.
2. Cut each breast into four strips. Sprinkle salt, pepper and paprika over chicken pieces. Dredge in flour.
3. In a medium mixing bowl, mix eggs with garlic. Dip chicken pieces in egg, making sure that any excess drips off. Transfer to plate.
4. In a large mixing bowl, blend together breadcrumbs, cornflake crumbs, sesame seeds and cheese. Coat chicken pieces in crumb mixture.
5. Place on baking sheet that has been sprayed with cooking spray. Bake for 10 minutes. Turn over and bake an additional 7 minutes or until chicken is no longer pink inside.

Dipping Sauces

The prepared kinds will do, but if you want to go that extra mile, try these sauces.

Sweet Mustard

This recipe yields 1 cup.

½ cup	Dijon mustard	½ cup	calorie-reduced maple syrup

Blend ingredients together with a wire whisk.

Plum Sauce

This recipe yields three to four cups.

2 lb	assorted red and purple plums, peeled, pitted and quartered	¼ cup	white sugar
1 lb	fresh apricots, peeled, pitted and quartered	2 tbsp	orange juice
¾ cup	light brown sugar	2 tsp	ground cinnamon
¾ cup	apple juice	1 tsp	grated lemon zest
		½ tsp	ground ginger
		½ tsp	ground allspice

1. In a large saucepan, bring all ingredients to a boil over medium heat. Reduce heat to simmer and cook, covered, for 1½ hours, stirring occasionally to break apart plums and apricots.
2. Place mixture in the work bowl of a food processor and process for 15 seconds, or until puréed.

Barbecue Sauce

This recipe yields about 1½ cups.

¾ cup	prepared barbecue sauce	3 tbsp	frozen apple juice concentrate, thawed
¼ cup	brown sugar	1 tsp	chili powder
¼ cup	ketchup	¼ tsp	salt

Blend all ingredients together with a wire whisk.

Fake Fries

These fries are just as delicious and more nutritious than their deep-fried counterparts. This recipe makes 4 dozen fries.

2 tbsp	canola oil
1 tsp	minced fresh garlic
6	baking potatoes, unpeeled and well scrubbed
	Salt, pepper and paprika

1. Preheat oven to 400°F.
2. In a small measuring cup with a spout, mix together oil and garlic. Set aside.
3. Cut each potato in half lengthwise. Cut each half in half lengthwise. Cut each quarter in half lengthwise, making eight wedges per potato.
4. Place wedges on a cookie sheet that has been sprayed with cooking spray. Drizzle with oil and garlic mixture. Sprinkle with salt, pepper and paprika.
5. Bake for 10 to 15 minutes. Flip wedges over and cook for another 10 to 15 minutes or until tender.

Mini Burgers

Each mini burger is just enough for two or three bites. This recipe makes 12 to 16 burgers.

2 lb	lean ground beef	1 tsp	minced fresh basil
½ cup	cornflake crumbs	1 tsp	Dijon mustard
1 tbsp	finely chopped onion	½ tsp	salt
1 tbsp	ketchup	½ tsp	pepper
1 tsp	minced fresh garlic	12–16	small dinner rolls

1. Preheat oven to broil.
2. Place ground beef, cornflake crumbs, onion, ketchup, garlic, basil, mustard, salt and pepper in the work bowl of a food processor. Process for 20 to 30 seconds or until well blended.
3. Shape into patties about ¼-inch thick and 2 to 3 inches in diameter. There should be 12 to 16 patties.
4. Place on cookie sheet that has been sprayed with cooking spray. Broil for about 5 minutes per side or until each side is browned. Insert into rolls.

Lemonade with Pint-Sized Fruit Kebabs

Despite its many commercial imitations, home-made lemonade is still a special treat. This recipe makes about 15 glasses.

8 cups	water
2 cups	white sugar
Juice of 10	lemons
Juice of 2	medium oranges
Grated zest of 3	lemons
Grated zest of 1	medium orange

Fruit Kebabs

15	pineapple chunks
15	mandarin orange sections
15	banana slices (each 1 inch thick)
15	cocktail toothpicks

1. In a large saucepan, bring 4 cups of the water and sugar to boil over medium-high heat, stirring until sugar is dissolved.
2. Reduce heat to simmer. Add lemon juice, orange juice, lemon zest and orange zest and stir until blended. Add remaining 4 cups water and simmer for another 2 to 3 minutes. Cool.
3. Transfer to a pitcher and refrigerate until chilled.
4. Thread one piece each of pineapple, orange and banana on a cocktail toothpick.
5. To serve, make a small cut into the pineapple piece of the kebab, enabling it to rest on the rim of a glass. Pour lemonade and serve.

Mad Apples

Some say that the apple is the earliest known fruit, having been found in the Garden of Eden. Virtually all apples are delicious on their own. The most popular are –

Red Delicious – deep red in colour, sweet taste
McIntosh – red and green in colour, sweet or tart taste
Granny Smith – pale green in colour, tart taste
Jonathan – bright red in colour, sweet or tart taste
Macoun – burgundy in colour, tart taste
Winesap – burgundy in colour, sweet or tart taste

Cooking apples should be firm and flavourful. Besides the Granny Smith and the Jonathan, which are excellent for cooking, there are –

Baldwin – various shades of red in colour, sweet taste
Northern Spy – pale yellow in colour, sweet or tart taste
Rome Beauty – deep red in colour, sweet taste

McIntosh apples are very good for applesauce, as they are soft and break down easily when heated.

The Privilege of Pears

After the apple, the pear is the second-most widely grown and consumed fruit.

Anjou – green to russet in colour, sweet flavour
Red Anjou – burgundy in colour, sweet flavour
Bartlett – large, bell shaped, yellow to green in colour, sweet flavour
Bosc – thin necked, brown and russet in colour, sweet and musky flavour, ideal for baking and cooking
Comice – large and round, very sweet flavour, excellent with cheese
Forelle – small, yellow with red flecks, sweet flavour
Seckel – tiny, burgundy and green in colour, very sweet flavour

Black and White Sandwiches

For a lighter treat, substitute low-fat frozen yogurt for the ice cream. This recipe makes 12 frozen treats.

24	chocolate wafers
2 cups	vanilla ice cream, softened

1. Place 12 wafers on a work surface. Top each one with 2 tbsp ice cream. Top with remaining cookies.
2. Place sandwiches on a cookie sheet and freeze for at least 2 hours or overnight.

Nuts to You

Nuts are the hard-shelled edible seeds of trees, bushes and other plants. They are high in nutritional content, full of protein and vitamin E.

Almonds – This nut is thin and oval shaped, with a thin brown skin that is peeled to produce blanched almonds; it is used in baked goods, pastas, stuffing.

Brazil nuts – This nut is moon shaped, with a woodlike shell, which, when cracked open, has 12 to 24 nuts inside. It is used in nut assortments.

Cashews – This nut is crescent shaped, with a sweet taste. It is used in baked goods and dressings.

Hazelnuts – This nut, also called the filbert, has a hard, brown shell, which is peeled to reveal its small, round, sweet flesh. Used in baked goods, it can also be ground into oil.

Macadamias – This nut has an extremely hard shell that is peeled to reveal its large, round, buttery-flavoured flesh. It is used in breads and salads.

Peanuts – This nut has a thin, light brown shell that is peeled to reveal two small nuts. It is the most popular snacking nut and its oil is used for cooking.

Pecans – This nut has a hard shell that is peeled to reveal its sweet flesh. It is used in baked goods and it goes well with chocolate.

Pine nuts (pignoli) – This nut, harvested from pine cones, is tiny and flavourful. It is excellent in salads and essential to pesto.

Pistachios – This nut has a thin white shell and pale green flesh. It is mostly eaten raw or in dessert toppings.

Walnuts – This nut has a hard shell with an irregular surface and mild-tasting flesh. It is used in baked goods.

The Birthday Cake

This recipe is written for two 9-inch cakes. To make a cake that spells out the name *Dave*, you will need to double this recipe to yield four cakes, one for each letter. You can easily satisfy 24 people with it.

2½ cups	cake and pastry flour
1¼ tsp	baking powder
1¼ tsp	baking soda
1 tsp	salt
1 tsp	ground cinnamon
½ tsp	nutmeg
1½ cups	white sugar
¾ cup	butter or stick-type low-fat margarine, softened
2	eggs
1 tsp	vanilla
¾ cup	1% milk

Icing and Decoration

4	squares (each 1 oz) unsweetened chocolate
½ cup	butter OR stick-type low-fat margarine, softened
3½ cups	icing sugar
¼–½ cup	1% or 2% milk
	Assorted candies (e.g., jelly beans, gum drops), one type for each cake

1. Preheat oven to 350°F.
2. Place flour, baking powder, baking soda, salt, cinnamon and nutmeg in a large mixing bowl and stir with a wooden spoon until thoroughly blended. Set aside.
3. Place sugar and butter in a large mixing bowl. Using an electric mixer, beat at medium speed until fluffy. Add eggs and vanilla and beat until smooth.
4. Reduce speed to low. Add dry ingredients alternately with the milk, making three additions of dry ingredients and two of milk, and beating until batter is smooth.
5. Pour batter into two 9-inch baking pans that have been sprayed with cooking spray. Bake for 30 to 35 minutes or until knife inserted comes out clean. Let cool.
6. Meanwhile cut a paper pattern for each of the block letters *D, A, V,* and *E.* Use a ruler for any straight edges. Make sure each letter is a little smaller than the 9-inch cake. Try to make the letters of uniform size.
7. Invert cakes onto a work surface that has been dusted with flour. (To continue with this recipe you will need two more cakes.)

8. Place each paper pattern on a cake. Carefully cut around the pattern with a serrated knife.
9. Gently transfer letters onto a large serving board or platter and arrange to spell out *Dave*. You may need a couple of large spatulas to assist you with this process.
10. To make icing, place chocolate in the top of a double boiler. Stir over simmering heat until chocolate is melted.
11. Place chocolate and butter in a medium mixing bowl. Using an electric mixer, beat at medium speed for 10 seconds. Add icing sugar and beat for another 10 seconds or until well blended.
12. In a small saucepan, bring milk to a boil over medium-high heat.
13. With mixer at medium speed, gradually add milk until icing is smooth and blended, 20 to 30 seconds.
14. Using a knife, spread the frosting evenly over the four cake letters.
15. Decorate each cake letter with a different type of candy.

Caramel Corn

This recipe feeds 12 munchers.

½ cup	stick-type low-fat margarine	½ tsp	salt
		½ tsp	vanilla
1 cup	brown sugar	½ tsp	baking soda
⅓ cup	light corn syrup	10 cups	popcorn

1. Preheat oven to 225°F.
2. In a medium saucepan, heat margarine over medium heat. Add brown sugar, corn syrup, salt and vanilla and stir until mixture reaches a boil, about 5 minutes.
3. Remove pan from heat and add baking soda. Place popcorn in a large mixing bowl. Pour brown sugar mixture over popcorn and toss to coat.
4. Place popcorn on two cookie sheets that have been sprayed with cooking spray. Bake for 1 to 1½ hours or until corn syrup and sugar have hardened, stirring every 20 minutes. Let cool.
5. Divide caramel corn into 12 portions. Place each portion in a small cellophane bag and tie with a decorative ribbon.

HAPPY HOUR

Happy hours are those times when people get together simply to relax, unwind and enjoy each other's company.

Instead of a meal, your guests are offered an array of finger foods, which usually become even more than a meal. Appetizers are the culinary fare of the happy hour. They can be passed around on trays or displayed on a buffet table.

Appetizers also work well as the culinary fare for the cocktail party that accompanies a book launch, a gallery or theatre opening or any other special occasion.

Menu

Serves 12

Sweet Potato Chips with Date Peach Chutney

Won Ton Chips with Spinach Dip and Red Pepper

Pumped-Up Portobellos

Endive Spears with Tuna Bean Spread

Dumplings with Nutty Ricotta Filling in Red Pepper Sauce

Strudel Filled with Wild Rice and Goat Cheese

Chicken and Beef Satay

Mini Frittatas

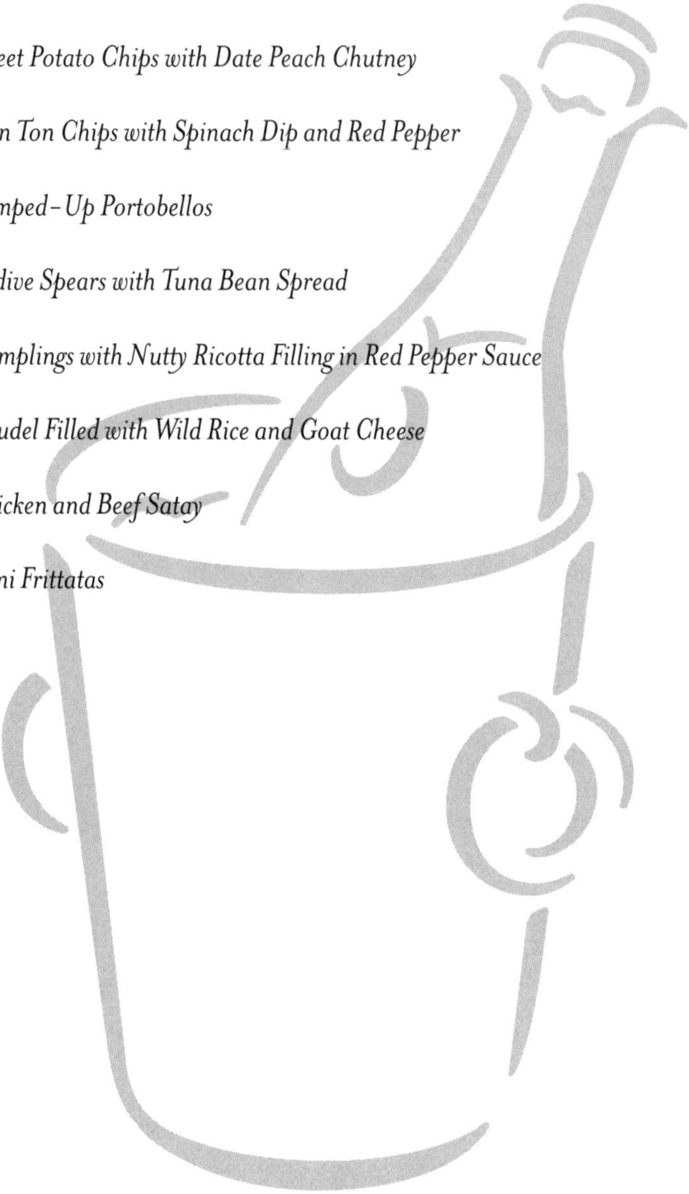

Presentation

Each appetizer should be served on its own platter. Line platters with radicchio, escarole or curly endive. Scatter some edible flowers on the platters for a splash of colour.

Serve the satays on their bamboo skewers. The dumplings can be picked up with cocktail toothpicks. Have lots of cocktail napkins on hand, as well as small forks at your guests' request.

You will not need a buffet table if you decide to simply pass around your appetizers. But if you decide to display the spread, make this simple centrepiece: Take three small terracotta flower pots, tie some raffia around each one and fill with candy, nuts, mandarin oranges or anything colourful and edible.

I suggest the following jazz selections for the musical accompaniment: *In a Silent Way* by Miles Davis, *The Art of John Coltrane* by John Coltrane and *The Best of Dizzy Gillespie* by Dizzy Gillespie.

Preparation Schedule

Fortunately, the fillings, dips and spreads can be made a day or two before.

Two Days Before

1. Make the Won Ton Chips and store them in an airtight container.
2. Make the Strudel Dough and refrigerate.
3. Make the Red Pepper Sauce and refrigerate.
4. Make the Date Peach Chutney and refrigerate.

The Day Before

1. Make the satay marinade and add chicken and beef. Refrigerate.
2. Make the Wild Rice and Goat Cheese Filling for the Strudel. Refrigerate.
3. Make the Tuna Bean Spread. Refrigerate.
4. Make the Nutty Ricotta Filling for the dumplings. Refrigerate.
5. Make the Spinach Dip for the Won Ton Chips. Refrigerate.
6. Make the filling for the Pumped-Up Portobellos. Refrigerate.
7. Construct the satays and refrigerate.

That Day

1. Preheat oven to 400°F.
2. Make the Sweet Potato Chips and bake for 12 minutes on each side.
3. While chips are baking, make frittatas and set aside.
4. Fill Endive Spears with the Tuna Bean Spread and arrange on platter.
5. Remove chips from the oven. Reduce heat to 375°F. Bake frittatas for 12 to 15 minutes.
6. While frittatas are baking, assemble the strudel. Remove frittatas and bake strudel for 15 to 20 minutes. Arrange frittatas on serving platter.
7. Make the dumplings. Place them without touching each other on a cornstarch-dusted surface.
8. Remove strudel from the oven. Let cool. Reduce heat to 350°F.
9. Spoon chutney onto Sweet Potato Chips and arrange on serving platter.

10. Cut up strudel and arrange pieces on a serving platter.
11. Assemble Pumped-Up Portobellos and bake for 20 minutes.
12. While they are baking, simmer the dumplings in a saucepan on the stove. Remove portobellos from the oven, top with feta cheese and arrange on a serving platter.
13. Place dumplings on a platter lined with Red Pepper Sauce.
14. Turn oven to broil (or heat up barbecue). Cook satays.

Sweet Potato Chips with Date Peach Chutney

Chutney is a relish made from fruits and spices. Use any leftover chutney as an accompaniment to chicken or turkey. This recipe makes about 24 chips and 2 cups chutney.

2	large sweet potatoes, peeled and cut into ⅛-inch slices
¼ cup	low-fat margarine, melted
	Salt and pepper

Date Peach Chutney

½ cup	white sugar
½ cup	brown sugar
¼ cup	apple cider vinegar
1 tsp	ground ginger
1 tsp	ground cinnamon
1 tsp	ground allspice
¼ tsp	ground cloves
1	small onion, finely chopped
½ tsp	minced fresh garlic
4	fresh peaches, cut in ½-inch dice
¼ cup	chopped dates

1. Preheat oven to 400°F.
2. Brush each sweet potato slice with margarine. Sprinkle with salt and pepper.
3. Place slices on a cookie sheet that has been lined with foil and then sprayed with cooking spray. Bake for about 12 minutes per side or until tender and lightly browned.
4. In a large saucepan, heat white and brown sugars, vinegar, ginger, cinnamon, allspice and cloves over medium-low heat. Whisk for 2 to 3 minutes.
5. Increase heat to medium high. Add onion and garlic and bring mixture to a boil. Add peaches and return to a boil.
6. Reduce heat to low. Cover and simmer for about 12 minutes or until thickened. Add dates and cook 10 minutes longer.
7. Place approximately 1 tbsp chutney on each chip.

Won Ton Chips with Spinach Dip and Red Pepper

This recipe makes 12 chips and about 2 cups dip. For another occasion make the Spinach Dip and serve it in a hollowed-out loaf of pumpernickel bread.

1 tbsp	olive oil
1 tsp	minced fresh garlic
12	won ton wrappers
12	thin strips roasted red pepper (from a jar)

Spinach Dip

2 cups	water
1 pkg	(10 oz) frozen spinach
½ cup	fat-free sour cream
½ cup	fat-free mayonnaise
3	green onions (green parts removed), thinly sliced
1 tbsp	chopped pimentos
1 tsp	minced fresh garlic

1. Preheat oven to 375°F.
2. In a small bowl, whisk together olive oil and garlic.
3. Place wrappers on a work surface that has been dusted with cornstarch. Brush with olive oil mixture.
4. Transfer wrappers to a cookie sheet that has been sprayed with cooking spray. Bake for 5 minutes or until crisp.
5. To make dip, in a medium saucepan bring water to a boil over high heat. Add spinach. Reduce heat to medium and cook for 5 minutes. Rinse under cold water. Drain and coarsely chop.
6. Place spinach, sour cream, mayonnaise, green onions, pimentos and garlic in a blender or the work bowl of a food processor. Process for 15 to 20 seconds or until blended.
7. Place approximately 1 tbsp dip on top of each chip. Top with a strip of roasted pepper.

Pumped-Up Portobellos

This recipe makes 12 appetizer portions.

1 tsp	olive oil
½ cup	cubed purple onion
2 tsp	minced fresh garlic
1 tbsp	minced fresh parsley
¼ cup	dry breadcrumbs
¼ cup	freshly grated Parmesan cheese
¾ cup	low-fat chicken broth
3	large portobello mushrooms, stems removed
3 tbsp	crumbled feta cheese

1. Preheat oven to 350°F.
2. In a medium skillet, heat oil over medium heat. Add onion and garlic and sauté for 2 to 3 minutes or until softened. Sprinkle with parsley and set aside.
3. In a medium bowl, mix together breadcrumbs and Parmesan cheese. Add onion mixture and mix thoroughly. Pour in ½ cup of the broth and mix together with a wooden spoon until blended.
4. Place mushrooms in a 9- x 11-inch baking dish that has been sprayed with cooking spray. Pour remaining ¼ cup broth into bottom of dish.
5. Place one-third of the breadcrumb mixture in each mushroom cap. Bake for 20 minutes or until mushrooms are tender.
6. Top each cap with 1 tbsp feta cheese. Carefully cut each cap into quarters.

Endive Spears with Tuna Bean Spread

This recipe makes 12 healthful treats.

2 cups	drained canned white beans
1 can	(7 oz) water-packed tuna, drained
⅓ cup	fat-free mayonnaise
1 tsp	minced fresh garlic
1 tsp	salt
1 tsp	pepper
1 tsp	lemon juice
12	endive spears
12 tsp	capers

1. Place beans, tuna, mayonnaise, garlic, salt, pepper and lemon juice in the work bowl of a food processor. Process for 10 to 15 seconds or until blended.
2. Place approximately 1 tbsp of the bean mixture in each endive spear. Top each spear with 1 tsp of the capers.

Dumplings with Nutty Ricotta Filling in Red Pepper Sauce

This recipe makes 18 dumplings.

1 tsp	cornstarch
¼ cup	water
18	won ton wrappers

Nutty Ricotta Filling

2 tsp	olive oil
½ cup	thinly sliced button mushrooms
¼ cup	pine nuts
1 cup	partly skimmed ricotta cheese
¼ cup	freshly grated Parmesan cheese
2	egg whites
1 tbsp	fresh minced basil

Red Pepper Sauce

1 tsp	olive oil
1	medium onion, cut in ¼-inch dice
2 tsp	minced fresh garlic
½ tsp	chili powder
1 can	(19 oz) plum tomatoes, undrained
3	medium red peppers, seeded and cut into ½-inch cubes
1 tbsp	white sugar
1 tbsp	balsamic vinegar
¼ cup	chopped fresh parsley
2 tbsp	freshly grated Parmesan cheese

1. To make filling, in a large saucepan, heat oil over medium heat. Add mushrooms and pine nuts and sauté for 2 to 3 minutes or until mushrooms are softened. Place in a large mixing bowl.
2. Add ricotta and Parmesan cheeses, egg whites and basil to the bowl. Blend mixture thoroughly with a fork.
3. To make sauce, in a large saucepan, heat oil over medium heat. Sauté onion and garlic for 2 to 3 minutes or until softened. Sprinkle with chili powder.
4. Add tomatoes, red peppers, sugar and vinegar. Bring to a boil and then reduce heat to low. Cover and simmer for 30 to 40 minutes or until peppers are soft. Add parsley and cheese and simmer for another 10 minutes.
5. Place sauce in the work bowl of a food processor and process for about 20 seconds or until thoroughly blended.
6. Dissolve cornstarch in water; set aside.
7. Slightly dampen each won ton wrapper by sprinkling it with a few drops of water. Place diagonally on a work surface that has been dusted with cornstarch.
8. Place a heaping teaspoon of filling in the middle of each wrapper.
9. Take bottom point of wrapper and fold over the mixture, lining up bottom point with top point.
10. Dip thumb and index fingers into cornstarch mixture. Seal edges, being sure to make an airtight seal. Repeat process until all wrappers are used. Place dumplings on a cookie sheet that has been dusted with cornstarch.
11. In a large skillet, bring 2 inches of water to a simmer over medium heat. With a slotted spoon, carefully lower dumplings in batches into the water. Simmer for about 5 minutes, or until dumplings appear soft.
12. Place 1 cup of the Red Pepper Sauce on a serving platter. Arrange dumplings on top.

Strudel Filled with Wild Rice and Goat Cheese

This recipe makes 2 rolls, each roll yielding 12 slices.

Strudel Dough

1½ cups	all-purpose flour
1 cup	cold butter OR stick-type low-fat margarine, cut in 1-inch chunks
½ cup	fat-free sour cream OR plain yogurt

Wild Rice and Goat Cheese Filling

2 cups	cooked wild rice
1½ cups	crumbled goat cheese
2 tbsp	chopped chives
2	egg whites, slightly beaten
2 tbsp	poppy or sesame seeds

1. Place flour and butter in a large mixing bowl. With a pastry cutter or with two knives, cut up the butter into little pieces until the mixture resembles coarse oatmeal.
2. Add sour cream. Blend with a fork until the dough forms a ball.
3. Divide the dough in half and wrap in plastic. Chill in refrigerator for at least 2 hours.
4. Preheat oven to 375°F.
5. On a floured surface, roll half the dough into a 9- x 12-inch rectangle.
6. Spread half of the rice over dough to within 1 inch of the edges. Sprinkle half of the goat cheese over top. Sprinkle half of the chives over top of cheese.
7. Brush egg whites on exposed edges. Fold in the edges and roll up jelly-roll style and pinch edge to seal.
8. Repeat steps 5 to 7 with remaining dough.
9. Transfer rolls to cookie sheet that has been sprayed with cooking spray. Cut small steam vents into the top of the roll. Brush tops with remaining egg white and sprinkle with seeds.
10. Bake for 15 to 20 minutes or until golden. Cool and cut each roll into 12 slices.

Chicken and Beef Satay

Satay is a classic example of Indonesian cuisine. Like shish kebab, it is served on skewers. Substitute three 6-ounce tuna steaks for the chicken and beef, if desired. This recipe makes 12 appetizers.

2 tbsp	lemon juice
2 tbsp	soy sauce
2 tsp	minced fresh garlic
1 tsp	minced fresh ginger
1 tsp	white sugar
2	boneless skinless chicken breasts (about ½ lb), each cut into thirds widthwise
½–¾ lb	boneless top sirloin or flank steak, cut diagonally into 6 strips
12	bamboo skewers

1. In a large mixing bowl, whisk together lemon juice, soy sauce, garlic, ginger and sugar.
2. Place chicken and beef strips in bowl and thoroughly coat with marinade. Cover and refrigerate for 4 hours or overnight, turning strips over occasionally.
3. Preheat oven to broil.
4. Thread one piece of chicken or beef on each skewer. Place skewers on a cookie sheet that has been sprayed with cooking spray.
5. Broil or grill for 5 to 7 minutes or until cooked through.

Mini Frittatas

These 12 little tarts give variety to the menu.

1 tsp	canola oil	3	egg whites
½ cup	cubed red pepper	½ tsp	salt
¼ cup	cubed purple onion	½ tsp	pepper
1 tsp	minced fresh garlic	¼ cup	shredded low-fat mozzarella cheese
¼ cup	black olives, coarsely chopped	2 tbsp	freshly grated Parmesan cheese
6	eggs		

1. Preheat oven to 375°F.
2. In a large skillet, heat oil over medium heat. Sauté red pepper, onion and garlic for 2 to 3 minutes or until softened. Add olives and stir until just blended.
3. Divide mixture equally amongst the mini muffin cups of a 12 cup tray that has been sprayed with cooking spray.
4. In a large mixing bowl, whisk together the eggs and egg whites. Add salt and pepper.
5. Pour egg mixture into muffin cups, being sure to distribute evenly.
6. Sprinkle mozzarella cheese over egg mixture. Top with Parmesan cheese.
7. Bake for 12 to 15 minutes or until egg is set.

Incredibly Edible Flowers

As an adornment to a serving platter, nothing is prettier than a flower. You can also add these edible flowers to your salads. This listing gives the colour of each flower to help you keep to a colour scheme.

Anise hyssop –	lavender
Apple blossom –	pink
Begonia –	red, yellow, pink, white
Borage –	lavender
Chive blossom –	lavender
Chrysanthemum –	white, yellow
Daisy –	white, yellow
Day lily –	orange, yellow, red
Geranium –	red, pink, white
Hollyhock –	pink, lavender
Johnny-jump-up –	white, yellow
Lavender –	lavender
Marigold –	yellow
Nasturtium –	yellow, orange
Pansy –	purple, white, yellow
Violet –	purple

Dip In

This Peanut Sauce enhances the flavour of dumplings and satays. For variety, also try Sweet Mustard, Plum Sauce and Barbecue Sauce (all p. 101). This recipe yields about one cup of sauce.

Peanut Sauce

½ cup	smooth peanut butter	2 tsp	minced fresh garlic
½ cup	soy sauce	¼ tsp	red pepper flakes
2 tbsp	rice vinegar	2 tbsp	sesame oil
1 tbsp	white sugar		

Place peanut butter, soy sauce, vinegar, sugar, garlic and red pepper flakes in the work bowl of a food processor and process for 10 seconds or until blended. While machine is running, add oil and process until well blended, about another 10 seconds.

THE GREAT OUTDOORS

Picture yourself sitting on a blanket spread out under the shade of a large tree. This tree could be located in a park, near the shoreline of a lake, at the foot of a mountain or simply in a backyard. Imagine being accompanied by your friends and a delightful array of food.

The picnic is a luxury in which we no longer indulge. It is one of those simple pleasures that seems to belong to a quieter, more genteel era.

Perhaps this next menu will inspire you to go back in time and have your own picnic, just for the fun of it.

Menu

Serves 12

Apple Carrot Slaw with Smoked Trout

Sweet Pea Penne Salad

Roasted New Potatoes Stuffed with Goat Cheese

Colourful Cornbread

Baby Drums

Meatball Tortellini Swords

Tuna Patties

Assorted Roll-Ups:

- *Turkey*
- *Smoked Salmon*
- *Beef*

Better Than Brownies

Peanut Butter Cookies

Presentation

You will need to transport your goodies. Bring several blankets, plastic table cloths and garbage bags. Fill one picnic basket with paper plates, plastic forks, napkins, towelettes, plastic cups and a corkscrew. Fill another basket with the cookies, cornbread and brownies. Fill one cooler just with drinks. Fill another cooler(s) with the slaw, penne salad, potatoes, swords, patties and roll ups. Bring a portable CD or tape player so that you may listen to the following rhythm and blues selections: *MTV Unplugged NYC 1997* by Babyface, *A Bit of Soul* by Aretha Franklin and *Songs in the Key of Life* by Stevie Wonder.

Preparation Schedule

One Week Before

1. Make the Colourful Cornbread. Wrap bread in foil. Place in plastic freezer bag. Freeze.
2. Make Better Than Brownies. Wrap in foil and place in freezer bag. Freeze.
3. Make the Peanut Butter Cookies. Place in an airtight container. Freeze.

The Day Before

1. Take cornbread, brownies and cookies out of the freezer.
2. Make the marinade for the Baby Drums and marinate them overnight.
3. Make the marinade for the steak for the Beef Roll-Ups and marinate it overnight.
4. Make the Sweet Pea Sauce and refrigerate.
5. Make the meatballs for the Meatball Tortellini Swords and refrigerate.
6. Make the Turkey Roll-Ups and the Smoked Salmon Roll-Ups and refrigerate.
7. Cut the cornbread and brownies into individual portions. Place in airtight containers.

That Day

1. Preheat oven to 350°F.
2. Make the Tuna Patties. Place on cookie sheet and set aside.
3. Put potatoes and Baby Drums in the oven. Bake the potatoes for 35 minutes and the drums for 1 hour.
4. Make Apple Carrot Slaw and place in an airtight container.
5. Remove potatoes from the oven.
6. Boil the tortellini for the Meatball Tortellini Swords and the penne for Sweet Pea Penne Salad. Drain and rinse.
7. Make the Sweet Pea Penne Salad. Place in an airtight container.

8. Refresh the tortellini with cold water and assemble the swords. Place in an airtight container.
9. Stuff potatoes with goat cheese and place in an airtight container.
10. Remove Baby Drums from the oven and bake Tuna Patties for 20 to 25 minutes.
11. Cut up Turkey and Smoked Salmon Roll-Ups. Place in airtight containers.
12. Remove patties from the oven. Raise heat to broil (or heat up the barbecue).
13. Broil beef and peppers for the Beef Roll-Ups. Put Drums and patties in containers. Put Roll-Ups in a container.

Apple Carrot Slaw with Smoked Trout

Coleslaw is the most traditional of salads. This variation is certainly not humdrum. This recipe yields 12 portions.

2	Granny Smith apples, peeled, cored and cut in ¼-inch cubes
1 tbsp	lemon juice
3 cups	shredded green cabbage
2	large carrots, cut diagonally into ¼-inch slices
1	medium red pepper, seeded and cut into matchsticks
2	smoked trout fillets (about 4 oz each), broken into small pieces
1	small bunch green onions (green parts removed), thinly sliced
2 tbsp	chopped fresh parsley

Dressing

¼ cup	fat-free mayonnaise
¼ cup	fat-free plain yogurt
3 tbsp	apple cider vinegar
1 tbsp	liquid honey
1 tsp	prepared mustard
¼ tsp	salt
¼ tsp	pepper

1. In a medium bowl, whisk together the dressing ingredients. Set aside.
2. Place the apples in a large mixing bowl. Sprinkle with lemon juice.
3. Add the cabbage, carrots, red pepper, trout, green onion and parsley to the bowl. Mix together with a wooden spoon.
4. Add the dressing to the slaw and mix thoroughly until blended.

Sweet Pea Penne Salad

You'll probably be able to eke out 12 appetizer portions.

4 cups	water
1 lb	penne

Sweet Pea Sauce

1 tbsp	olive oil **OR** low-fat margarine
½ cup	cubed onions
1 tbsp	minced fresh garlic
3 cups	plus 2 tbsp vegetable broth
2 cups	fresh peas, pods removed
¼ cup	low-fat cream cheese
½ tsp	salt
½ tsp	pepper
2 tbsp	freshly grated Parmesan cheese

1. In a large saucepan, bring water to a boil.
2. Add the penne and boil until al dente, about 7 minutes.
3. Drain. Rinse under cold water and drain. Set aside.
4. In a medium saucepan, heat oil over medium heat. Add onions and garlic and sauté for about 3 minutes or until softened.
5. Add vegetable broth and bring to a boil. Add peas. Reduce heat to simmer and cook for about 10 minutes
6. Transfer to the work bowl of a food processor. Add cream cheese, salt and pepper. Process for about 20 seconds or until well blended.
7. In a large skillet, heat the remaining 2 tbsp broth over medium heat. Add penne and sweet pea sauce and sauté until well blended. Sprinkle with Parmesan cheese before serving.

Roasted New Potatoes Stuffed with Goat Cheese

This recipe makes 12 little treats.

12	small new potatoes, unpeeled		Salt and pepper
			Paprika
1 tbsp	olive oil	¼ cup	goat cheese

1. Preheat oven to 350°F.
2. Place potatoes in a 9- x 11-inch baking dish that has been sprayed with cooking spray. Drizzle with oil. Sprinkle with salt, pepper and paprika.
3. Bake for 35 to 45 minutes or until fork tender.
4. Cut a small slice off the bottom of each potato so that it will sit on a platter. With a melon baller or small knife, scoop out about half the pulp of each potato.
5. Stuff each one with 1 tsp cheese.

Colourful Cornbread

Fragrant and filling, this cornbread can also be used to as stuffing for roast turkey. This recipe serves 12.

2 tbsp	vegetable or low-fat chicken broth	¼ cup	white sugar
¼ cup	cubed red pepper	1 tbsp	baking powder
¼ cup	cubed yellow pepper	¼ tsp	salt
¼ cup	cubed green pepper	¼ tsp	pepper
¼ cup	cooked corn	1 cup	buttermilk
1 cup	all-purpose flour	¼ cup	canola oil
1 cup	yellow cornmeal	1	egg
		2 egg	whites

1. Preheat oven to 425°F.
2. In a large skillet, heat broth over medium heat. Add peppers and corn and sauté for 2 minutes or until softened. Set aside.
3. In a large mixing bowl, mix flour, cornmeal, sugar, baking powder salt and pepper with a wooden spoon until thoroughly blended.
4. In a medium mixing bowl, place buttermilk, oil, egg and egg whites. Using an electric mixer, blend at medium-high speed for 2 minutes.
5. With a wooden spoon, stir buttermilk mixture into dry ingredients until just blended. Stir in corn mixture.
6. Pour into 9- x 13-inch baking dish that has been sprayed with cooking spray. Bake for 25 minutes or until slightly brown on top. Cut into 12.

Baby Drums

The thick part of the chicken wing resembles a small drumstick. Reserve the other wing pieces for another use, such as Chicken Fricassee (p. 172). This recipe makes 18 drumlets.

3/4 cup	soy sauce
1/4 cup	orange juice
1/4 cup	brown sugar
3 tbsp	dry cooking sherry
1 tbsp	minced fresh garlic
1 tsp	minced fresh ginger
1/4 cup	olive oil
18	chicken drumlets
	Salt and pepper

1. Place soy sauce, orange juice, sugar, sherry, garlic and ginger in a large mixing bowl. Stir with a wire whisk until thoroughly blended. Whisk in olive oil.
2. Sprinkle drumlets with salt and pepper. Transfer to the mixing bowl and marinate, covered, overnight, turning drumlets over occasionally.
3. Preheat oven to 350°F. Place drumlets in a 9- x 11-inch baking dish that has been sprayed with cooking spray.
4. Bake for 1 hour, turning pieces over halfway and basting occasionally with sauce. Drumlets are done when no longer pink inside.

Meatball Tortellini Swords

Have bamboo skewers on hand for these items. This recipe provides 12 appetizer servings.

4 cups	water	12	cherry tomatoes
24	frozen chicken tortellini	12	bamboo skewers
1	recipe Some Spicy Meatballs (p. 53)		

1. In a large saucepan, bring water to a boil over high heat. Add tortellini. Reduce heat to medium low and cook for 10 to 12 minutes or until cooked through. Drain. Rinse under cold water and set aside.
2. On each skewer, thread one meatball, two tortellini and one cherry tomato.

Panzanella

Besides its taste, the best feature of this Tuscan tomato-and-bread salad is its convenient use of day-old bread. It would be a welcomed addition to a picnic. This recipe yields 12 portions.

6	slices day-old Italian bread, cut into ½-inch cubes	¼ cup	minced fresh basil
6	medium tomatoes, cut into ½-inch cubes	¼ cup	chopped fresh parsley
½	medium cucumber, peeled and cut into ½-inch cubes	¼ cup	olive oil
		1 small	purple onion, cut into ½-inch cubes
		1 tbsp	minced fresh garlic
		1 tsp	pepper
		½ tsp	salt

Place all ingredients in a large mixing bowl and stir until thoroughly mixed. Serve at room temperature.

Tuna Patties

This recipe yields 6 large or 12 small patties. Try substituting crab or salmon for the tuna.

1 tsp	canola oil
1	small bunch green onions (green parts removed), thinly sliced
½ tsp	minced fresh garlic
2	cans (each 7 oz) water-packed tuna, drained
1 cup	Italian-style breadcrumbs
2	egg whites
½ tsp	dry mustard
½ tsp	chili powder

1. Preheat oven to 350°F.
2. In a medium saucepan, heat oil over medium heat. Add onions and garlic and sauté for 2 to 3 minutes or until softened.
3. Transfer to a large mixing bowl. Add tuna, breadcrumbs, egg whites, mustard and chili powder and mix with a wooden spoon until thoroughly blended.
4. Form tuna mixture into patties. Place on a cookie sheet that has been sprayed with cooking spray.
5. Bake for 20 to 25 minutes (or until golden) for the large patties or 12 to 15 minutes for the small patties.

Assorted Roll-Ups

Turkey Roll-Ups

Substitute any of your favourite deli meats for the turkey. For a heartier variation, place a slice of cheddar cheese between the turkey and pear slices. This recipe yields 12 roll-ups.

3	large round slices roast turkey (from the deli)	1 tbsp	fat-free mayonnaise
1 tbsp	honey mustard	2	pears, each cut into 6 slices

1. Place turkey slices on a work surface. Brush each slice with 1 tsp of the mustard and 1 tsp of the mayonnaise.
2. Line up four pear slices on top of each turkey slice.
3. Roll up each slice jelly-roll style and wrap in plastic wrap. Refrigerate for 2 to 4 hours or overnight.
4. To serve, cut each roll in four slices and skewer each slice with a toothpick.

Smoked Salmon Roll-Ups

This recipe produces 12 roll-ups.

12	slices smoked salmon (about 1 lb)
¾ cup	low-fat cream cheese
2 tbsp	minced fresh dill
½ cup	capers

1. Line up smoked salmon slices on a work surface. Spread 1 tbsp of the cream cheese on each slice. Top with ½ tsp of the minced dill. Put a few capers in the middle of each slice.
2. Roll up each slice jelly-roll style and secure with a toothpick.

Beef Roll-Ups

Another tasty roll-up. Chicken or veal slices work as well. This recipe makes 12 roll-ups.

1½–2 lb	boneless top sirloin or flank steak
3	medium red or yellow peppers
6 tsp	chopped fresh parsley

Marinade

2 tbsp	olive oil
1 tbsp	minced fresh garlic
1 tbsp	soy sauce
1 tsp	liquid honey

1. In a small bowl, whisk marinade ingredients together.
2. Place steak in a shallow baking dish and pour marinade over top. Cover and refrigerate for 4 hours or overnight, turning steak over occasionally.
3. Preheat oven to broil.
4. Remove cores and seeds from peppers. Cut each pepper in half lengthwise. Cut each piece in half again lengthwise, to make 12 pieces.
5. Place steak on the barbecue or under the broiler on a cookie sheet that has been sprayed with cooking spray. Grill or broil for 3 or 4 minutes per side. Cut into twelve ½-inch strips. Set aside.
6. Grill or broil pepper pieces until the skins are charred black, about 2 to 3 minutes. Peel off the black skin and discard.
7. Place strips of beef on a work surface. Place one piece of pepper on top of each beef slice. Sprinkle ½ tsp parsley on top.
8. Roll up and fasten with a toothpick.

Better Than Brownies

This is my favourite recipe of the entire brownie repertoire. These brownies appeal to kids of all ages. This recipe yields 12 to 24 squares.

½ cup	butter OR low-fat margarine	2	eggs
2	squares (each 1 oz) unsweetened chocolate	1 tsp	vanilla
1 cup	white sugar	1	can (14 oz) low-fat sweetened condensed milk
½ cup	all-purpose flour	1 cup	graham cracker crumbs
½ tsp	baking powder	¾ cup	chocolate chips

1. Preheat oven to 350°F.
2. In a microwaveable bowl, combine butter and chocolate and microwave, uncovered, on high for 2 to 3 minutes or until mixture has melted. Set aside. Or melt the butter in a small saucepan and the chocolate in a double boiler; combine.
3. Place sugar, flour and baking powder in the work bowl of a food processor. Process for 10 seconds. While the machine is running, add eggs, vanilla and chocolate mixture and process until blended, about 10 seconds.
4. Add milk, graham cracker crumbs and chocolate chips to the work bowl. Process for 20 seconds.
5. Pour into a 9- x 11-inch baking dish that has been sprayed with cooking spray. Bake for 35 minutes or until a crust is formed on the top.
6. Cool and cut into squares.

Peanut Butter Cookies

This recipe yields about 2 dozen cookies.

2¾ cups	all-purpose flour	⅔ cup	calorie-reduced smooth peanut butter
½ tsp	baking soda	⅓ cup	brown sugar
½ tsp	baking powder	1	egg
¼ tsp	salt	1 tsp	vanilla
1 cup	white sugar	½ cup	unsalted, shelled peanuts
1 cup	butter OR stick-type, low-fat margarine, softened	½ cup	peanut butter chips

1. In a large mixing bowl, mix together first flour, baking soda, baking powder and salt until thoroughly blended. Set aside.
2. Place white sugar, butter, peanut butter and brown sugar in a mixing bowl. Using an electric mixer, beat at medium speed until light and fluffy. Add egg and vanilla and beat for another 10 seconds.
3. Gradually add dry ingredients, mixing with a wooden spoon until well blended. Add peanuts and peanut butter chips to the dough. Chill dough in the refrigerator for at least 1 hour.
4. Preheat oven to 375°F.
5. Shape dough into 1-inch balls. Place about 1-inch apart on a cookie sheet that has been sprayed with cooking spray. Press down each ball with the tines of a fork. Bake for 10 to 12 minutes, or until lightly browned.

Other Picnic Favourites

Mushroom Tarts

This recipe makes about 12 small tarts.

½ cup	olive oil	1	medium Spanish onion, cut into ½-inch dice
2 tsp	balsamic vinegar	1 cup	thinly sliced button mushrooms
1 tbsp	minced fresh garlic	½	recipe Strudel Dough (p.120)
¼ tsp	red pepper flakes		
¼ tsp	salt		

1. In a medium saucepan, heat oil, vinegar, garlic, red pepper flakes and salt over medium-high heat. Stir in onions and cook until wilted, about 5 minutes.
2. Place mushrooms in a large mixing bowl. Pour onion mixture over mushrooms. Cover and refrigerate overnight.
3. On a floured surface, roll out dough into a 9- x 12-inch rectangle. Using a 3-inch cookie cutter, cut out nine or ten circles.
4. Place dough circles in cups of a mini muffin tray that has been sprayed with cooking spray. Pat circle in the bottom and up the sides with your fingers. Gather up scraps of dough, reroll and cut out another couple of circles if possible. Cover tray and refrigerate for 1 hour. Preheat oven to 425°F.
5. To prevent bubbling during baking, line each tart with a circle of foil. Use a few dried beans in each cup as a weight.
6. Bake for 10 to 12 minutes or until edges are browned. Cool.
7. Remove tarts from tray. Stir mushroom filling well. Fill each tart with about 1 tbsp of the filling.

MIDNIGHT MADNESS

Midnight brunches usually wrap up a festive party or some other form of celebration. When I was a teenager, some poor, unsuspecting parent would offer to make this feast in the early hours of the morning for the prom goers.

New Year's Eve is actually the best time for this feast. After all, midnight is the peak of excitement on this special occasion and everyone can sleep in the next day.

Menu

Serves 12

Crudités and Dip

Baby Spinach with Grilled Pineapple,
Grilled Sweet Potato and Roasted Beets

Beggar's Purses

The Omelette Bar

Polenta Casserole

Risotto Cakes

Fun-Filled Strawberries

Perfect Peach Tarts

Presentation

Your everyday dishes and silverware will suffice for this buffet. Arrange the platters of spinach salad, crudités and dip, Risotto Cakes and Beggar's Purses on the table. Put the Polenta Casserole in its wicker basket. Display the tarts and strawberries on pedestal cake plates.

Set up your Omelette Bar in the kitchen. Encourage your guests to go into the kitchen after they have made their buffet selections. You will then make their customized omelette.

Since it is night-time, create a dramatic atmosphere by setting up the buffet in a darkened room. Dim the lights. Place tea lights in small glass jars in any empty spaces on the table. For the centrepiece, place a few persimmons in a glass trifle bowl. Surround it with tea lights. Sprinkle the table with gold and silver confetti.

Play the following musical selections: *Back to Front* by Lionel Richie, *Aja* by Steely Dan and *Silk Degrees* by Boz Scaggs.

Preparation Schedule

The Day Before

1. Make the crêpes for the Beggar's Purses. Put a sheet of wax paper between crêpes and put entire bundle into a large resealable plastic bag. Refrigerate.
2. Cut up the vegetables for the crudités and place in resealable plastic bags. Make the dip. Refrigerate.
3. Make the Sweet Fruit Rub and the Raspberry Vinaigrette. Refrigerate the vinaigrette.
4. Cook the sweet potatoes for the spinach salad and the Sweet Potato Filling. Refrigerate.
5. Roast the beets for the spinach salad. Refrigerate.
6. Make the Perfect Peach Tarts and place in an airtight container.
7. Assemble the Polenta Casserole. Wrap in foil and refrigerate.
8. Assemble all the filling ingredients for the Omelette Bar and place in individual airtight containers in the refrigerator.

That Day

1. Make the risotto. Refrigerate.
2. Make the Sweet Potato Filling. Set aside.
3. Make the Fun-Filled Strawberries. Refrigerate.
4. Turn oven to broil (or heat up the barbecue). Coat pineapple and sweet potato slices with Sweet Fruit Rub. Broil or grill. Lower heat to 350°F.
5. Make spinach salad and arrange on a serving platter with the pineapple and sweet potato slices and the beets.
6. Bake the Polenta Casserole for 30 minutes.
7. Make the Beggar's Purses. Arrange on serving platter.
8. Remove casserole from the oven. Arrange strawberries, tarts, and crudités and dip on serving platters.
9. Make the Risotto Cakes. Arrange on a serving platter.
10. Put out fillings for the Omelette Bar.

Crudités and Dip

The term *crudité* literally means "rawness" in French. This recipe will provide appetizer portions for a party of 12.

12	cucumber slices
12	green pepper slices
12	red pepper slices
12	yellow pepper slices
12	carrot sticks
12	celery sticks

Dip

2 cups	fat-free plain yogurt
2 tbsp	diced red pepper
1 tbsp	chopped chives
1 tsp	minced fresh garlic

1. Place dip ingredients in a mixing bowl and blend thoroughly with a wooden spoon. Transfer to a serving bowl. Chill for 1 hour or overnight.
2. Arrange vegies attractively on a platter, with the dip in the centre.

Baby Spinach with Grilled Pineapple, Grilled Sweet Potato and Roasted Beets

Try serving this salad for 12 in two hollowed-out pineapple halves and place them on either end of the buffet table.

½	pineapple, peeled and sliced into ½-inch rounds
2	boiled, peeled sweet potatoes, sliced into ½-inch rounds
2	large beets, tops removed
5 cups	baby spinach

Sweet Fruit Rub

2½ tbsp	brown sugar
½ tsp	ground cinnamon
¼ tsp	nutmeg

Raspberry Vinaigrette

3 tbsp	dry white wine
2 tbsp	orange juice
2 tbsp	olive oil
1 tbsp	minced chives
1 tbsp	raspberry-flavoured vinegar
1 tsp	liquid honey

1. Mix together ingredients for the rub and sprinkle evenly on a sheet of wax paper.
2. Lightly dip each side of each pineapple and sweet potato slice into rub mixture.
3. Grill on barbecue over medium heat or broil in oven for about 2 minutes per side or until browned.
4. Whisk all vinaigrette ingredients together in a small bowl. Set aside.
5. Preheat oven to 400°F.
6. Wrap each beet in foil and roast for 1 hour and 15 minutes or until tender.
7. Cool, peel and slice beets into ¼-inch rounds.
8. Place spinach in a large serving bowl. Toss with Raspberry Vinaigrette. Transfer to serving platter.
9. Overlap slices of pineapple, sweet potato and beets decoratively on top of the spinach.

Beggar's Purses

This recipe makes 12 of the prettiest hors d'oeuvres.

1	recipe Crêpe It Yourself (p.91)
12	long chives

Sweet Potato Filling

4 cups	water
2	sweet potatoes, peeled and cut in chunks
2 tbsp	low-fat margarine, melted
1 tbsp	brown sugar
1 tbsp	fat-free sour cream

1. In a large saucepan, make filling: bring water to a boil over high heat. Add sweet potatoes. Reduce heat to medium low. Cover and cook for about 20 minutes or until fork tender.
2. Pass chunks through a potato ricer and into a large mixing bowl. Add margarine, brown sugar and sour cream, and blend together with a wooden spoon.
3. Place 1 tbsp filling in the middle of each crêpe.
4. Gather up the edges of the crêpe to form a pouch. Secure pouch by tying it with a chive just above the filling.

The Omelette Bar

Eggs, the original comfort food, are an economical and nutritious source of protein and vitamin B_{12}. Unfortunately, the yolks are high in cholesterol. If cholesterol is a problem, use only the whites in your omelette. This recipe makes an omelette for one. You will need 3 dozen eggs for a party of 12.

3	eggs
	Salt and pepper
1 tsp	butter OR low-fat margarine
½ cup	omelette fillings (see below)

1. In a large bowl, beat eggs together with a wire whisk. Sprinkle with salt and pepper.
2. In an 8-inch skillet, heat butter over medium-high heat. Tilt the pan and swirl the butter so that it coats the entire pan.
3. Reduce heat to medium low. Pour in the eggs all at once. Spread them out evenly over the pan. Cook for about 10 seconds or until the bottom is set.
4. Using a spatula, lift up the omelette slightly, allowing the runny, uncooked egg to fall onto the surface of the pan. Repeat this technique until all the egg is cooked.
5. Turn heat off. Place filling in the centre of the omelette. Carefully fold the omelette in half with the spatula and slide onto a plate.

Omelette Fillings

Use these items by themselves or in combination:

salsa
shredded cheese
cubed avocado
cooked vegies, e.g., broccoli, spinach, potatoes, mushrooms, onions, peppers, zucchini
fresh herbs
cooked chicken or turkey
smoked salmon
salami

Polenta Casserole

Originally, the word *casserole* denoted the dish in which the food was cooked, rather than the food itself. Not only sturdy and ovenproof, a good casserole dish must also be attractive enough to be brought to the table. This recipe yields 12 small portions.

1 tsp	canola oil
1 cup	cubed onions
1 cup	cubed zucchini
1 cup	thinly sliced button mushrooms
2 tsp	minced fresh garlic
1 cup	niçoise olives, thinly sliced
1 cup	drained oil-packed sun-dried tomatoes, cut into ½-inch pieces
1 cup	prepared polenta
½ cup	all-purpose flour
½ cup	freshly grated Parmesan cheese
1 tbsp	minced fresh basil
½ tsp	salt
½ tsp	pepper
2 cups	1% or 2% milk
2	eggs
2	egg whites
¾ cup	shredded low-fat mozzarella cheese

1. Preheat oven to 350°F.
2. In a large skillet, heat oil over medium heat. Sauté onions, zucchini, mushrooms and garlic, for 2 to 3 minutes or until softened. Transfer to a large mixing bowl. Add olives and sun-dried tomatoes. Set aside.
3. In a large mixing bowl, blend together polenta, flour, Parmesan cheese, basil, salt and pepper until thoroughly mixed. Set aside.
4. In another large mixing bowl, whisk together milk, eggs and egg whites. Add polenta mixture and stir until thoroughly blended. Add onion mixture and stir.
5. Pour entire mixture into a 3-quart casserole dish that has been sprayed with cooking spray. Sprinkle cheese over top.
6. Bake, uncovered, for 30 minutes or until cheese is bubbly and golden.

Risotto Cakes

This recipe makes roughly 12 little cakes.

3–4 cups	vegetable or low-fat chicken broth	1 cup	freshly grated Parmesan cheese
1 tbsp	olive oil	1 tbsp	chopped fresh parsley
¾ cup	chopped purple onion		Salt and pepper
2 tsp	minced fresh garlic	2 tbsp	all-purpose flour
1½ cups	Arborio rice	3 tsp	canola oil
¾ cup	dry white wine		

1. In a medium saucepan, bring broth to a simmer over medium heat. Reduce heat to low and let stand until ready for use.
2. In a large skillet, heat oil over medium heat. Sauté onion and garlic for 2 to 3 minutes or until softened.
3. Add rice to skillet and cook, stirring, for 2 minutes or until the rice turns opaque.
4. Reduce heat to medium-low. Add ¼ cup of the wine to the skillet and stir until it is absorbed by the rice. Repeat this step twice more.
5. Add ½ cup of the broth to the rice and stir until absorbed. Continue to add broth in ¼-cup increments, allowing broth to be absorbed each time. Ultimately the grains should be tender yet firm, and the mixture should be creamy.
6. Sprinkle cheese and parsley over top and stir until just blended. Add salt and pepper to taste.
7. Put the risotto in a 9- x 13-inch glass baking dish that has been sprayed with cooking spray and refrigerate at least 1 hour.
8. Shape chilled risotto into flat cakes. Dip them in flour. Place them on a sheet of wax paper that has been dusted with cornstarch.
9. In a large skillet, heat 1 tsp of the oil over medium heat. Sauté one batch of the cakes for 3 minutes per side. Repeat with the remaining 2 tsp oil and cakes.

Fun-Filled Strawberries

If you don't have strawberries, pitted apricots work well. This recipe makes 12 to 16 strawberries.

1 quart	fresh strawberries, stems removed	¼ cup	mini white chocolate chips
2	containers (each 6 oz) fat-free strawberry yogurt		

1. Cut a small piece off the bottom of each strawberry so that it can stand upright on a serving platter.
2. With a melon baller, scoop out the pulp from each strawberry, leaving the shells intact.
3. Place pulp in a blender and blend for 10 seconds. Add yogurt and blend thoroughly.
4. With a small spoon, fill each hollowed-out strawberry with yogurt mixture. Place a few chocolate chips on top of each strawberry.

How to Make Your Own Polenta

Polenta, which is made from cornmeal, has the consistency of thick porridge. It originated in Northern Italy.

Replace lasagne noodles with polenta. Serve individual portions of polenta topped with sautéed vegetables as a first course or appetizer.

6 cups	vegetable or low fat chicken broth	1 tbsp	minced fresh garlic
2 tbsp	olive oil	1 tsp	salt
		2 cups	yellow cornmeal

1. In a large saucepan, heat broth, oil, garlic and salt over medium-high heat. Bring to a boil.
2. Reduce heat to medium low. Gradually add cornmeal, whisking constantly, until polenta is very thick, about 15 minutes.

Perfect Peach Tarts

The English began to use the word *tart* in the fourteenth century to denote an open pastry shell with a sweet and usually fruity filling. Substitute strawberries, blueberries, raspberries, nectarines or pears for peaches, if you'd like. This recipe makes 12 tarts.

2 cups	all-purpose flour
2 tsp	white sugar
½ tsp	ground cinnamon
½ tsp	salt
½ cup	cold or frozen stick-type low-fat margarine, cut in chunks
¼ cup	cold or frozen shortening, cut in chunks
½ cup	ice water
2 tbsp	graham cracker crumbs

Peach Filling

5 cups	thinly sliced fresh peaches, unpeeled
½ cup	white sugar
¼ cup	brown sugar
1 tsp	ground cinnamon
¼ cup	cornstarch
1 tbsp	lemon juice
1 tbsp	peach schnapps (optional)

1. Place flour, sugar, cinnamon and salt into the work bowl of food processor. Process for 1 minute.
2. Add margarine and shortening and process for another minute or until mixture resembles coarse oatmeal.
3. With machine running, add ice water through the feed tube and process until dough forms a ball.
4. Divide dough in half, wrap each half in plastic wrap and refrigerate while peach filling is being made.
5. To make filling, in a large mixing bowl gently mix together peaches, white and brown sugars and cinnamon with a wooden spoon.
6. Add cornstarch and blend thoroughly.
7. Add lemon juice and schnapps, if using, and stir again. Set aside.
8. Preheat oven to 425°F.
9. On a floured surface, roll each ball of dough into an approximately 11-inch circle. Using a 4-inch round cookie cutter, cut six rounds out of each dough, making 12 rounds all together.
10. Fit rounds into the cups of a 12-cup muffin pan that has been sprayed with cooking spray.
11. Sprinkle graham cracker crumbs into cups.
12. Spoon peach filling into cups.
13. Bake for 20 minutes.

Fruit Cocktail Pops

Another possibility for the Midnight Buffet, this recipe yields 12 to 15 nutritious frozen treats.

1 can	(12½ oz) frozen orange juice concentrate, thawed
1 can	(12½ oz) frozen apple juice concentrate, thawed
½ cup	drained canned sliced peaches
½ cup	drained canned pineapple chunks
4 cups	fat-free plain yogurt
12–15	small paper cups
12–15	wooden Popsicle sticks

1. Place orange and apple juice concentrates, peaches and pineapple in the work bowl of a food processor. Process for 10 seconds. Add yogurt and process for another 7 to 10 seconds or until blended.
2. Spoon mixture into paper cups, filling them almost to the top. Cover the top of each cup with a small piece of plastic wrap.
3. Using a knife, make a slit in the centre of the plastic wrap and insert the Popsicle stick.
4. Place cups in freezer and freeze until solid, about 4 hours or overnight.
5. To serve, remove plastic and peel away paper cup.

Tropical Delights

Grown in the tropical climates of Hawaii, the Caribbean Islands, Southeast Asia, Mexico, Central America and the Mediterranean region, these fruits have their own special appeal.

Avocado – Called the alligator pear because of its rough skin, it is high in protein and potassium.

Banana – Bland and easily digested, it is high in potassium and vitamin B_6.

Breadfruit – Large, green and spherical, it is a starchy fruit with the texture of a potato.

Coconut – The seed of the palm tree, it is used for its oil in shortening, shampoos and soap. Its inner flesh is eaten raw or shredded and used in baked goods.

Date – The sweet fruit of the date palm, it is high in potassium, sugar and iron.

Fig – Flower receptacles, pollinated by a specific type of wasp; are rich in magnesium, potassium, calcium and iron.

Guava – Pear shaped with deep pink flesh, it is an excellent source of vitamin C.

Mango – Large and pear shaped with sweet, yellow to orange flesh, it is an excellent source of beta carotene and vitamin C.

Papaya – Also pear shaped with sweet, yellow to orange flesh, it has black seeds, which are discarded. It is also high in beta carotene and vitamin C.

Pineapple – Large with a brown prickly skin, it has yellow flesh that is sweet and juicy. It is rich in vitamin B_6, and iron.

Plantain – Resembling a large green banana, it is served cooked as a side dish and is rich in vitamin A.

Pomegranate – Red in colour and spherical in shape, it is filled with deep red seeds.

Ugli fruit – Resembling a discoloured grapefruit, it is a hybrid of a grapefruit and a tangerine.

FAMILY UNITY

Parents, grandparents, sons, daughters, sisters, brothers, uncles, aunts, nieces, nephews and cousins all have one thing in common: they are all members of a family.

The meal becomes the focal point for the exchange of information, spirited discussions and laughter.

Menu

Serves 12

Carrot Raisin Salad

Spicy Noodle Salad

Focaccia with Onion and Garlic

Beef Tenderloin

Pan-Seared Tuna with Three Relishes:

- *Vegie Relish*
- *Don't Hold the Anchovies*
- *Black Bean Sauce*

Potato Croquettes

Zucchini Boats Stuffed with Hummus

Bread Pudding

Presentation

Use your good set of dishes, silverware and cloth napkins for the family event. After all, this type of gathering may not happen too often.

Place the Carrot Raisin Salad in a large wooden or ceramic salad bowl. The relishes can be displayed in three soup bowls. The Spicy Noodle Salad, tuna, croquettes and Zucchini Boats should be put on platters. Cut up the focaccia. Keep it warm in a bread basket lined with a colourful cloth napkin. Place the tenderloins on a cutting board and cut individual slices right at the table.

Clear the table off after dinner. Bring out the Bread Pudding and set it down in its wicker basket. Bring out bowls of grapes and tangerines. Make cappuccino.

Take some framed family pictures off the shelf. Put them in the middle of the table as a centrepiece.

Play the following box set for your guests: *Hitsville U.S.A: The Motown Singles Collection 1959–1971.*

Preparation Schedule

The Day Before

1. Soak the raisins and cranberries for the Bread Pudding overnight.
2. Make the three relishes for the Pan-Seared Tuna and store in airtight containers in the refrigerator.
3. Make the hummus for the Zucchini Boats. Refrigerate.
4. Season the tuna and refrigerate.
5. Make the marinade for the Beef Tenderloin and marinate overnight.
6. Make the dressing for the noodle salad and transfer to a jar. Refrigerate.
7. Make the Carrot Raisin Salad, place in an airtight container and refrigerate.
8. Prepare the Zucchini Boats and put them in a large resealable plastic bag. Refrigerate.

That Day

1. Preheat oven to 400°F. Proof the yeast for the focaccia.
2. Toast the bread cubes for the Bread Pudding.
3. Boil the potatoes for the croquettes. Remove bread cubes from oven.
4. While the potatoes are boiling, make the focaccia dough.
5. Drain the potatoes and prepare the croquettes. Set aside until ready to be sautéed.
6. Make the noodle salad. Preheat the oven to 350°F.
7. Make the Bread Pudding and bake for 45 minutes.
8. Prepare the focaccia.
9. Sauté croquettes and transfer to a platter.
10. Take Bread Pudding out of the oven and bake Zucchini Boats for 20 minutes.
11. Heat up Black Bean Sauce and put relishes and salads out on the table.
12. Take Zucchini Boats out of the oven. Raise heat to 475°F. Bake focaccia for 20 minutes.
13. Stuff Zucchini Boats with hummus and arrange on platter.
14. Take focaccia out of the oven. Lower heat to 375°F. Bake tenderloin for 35 to 45 minutes.
15. While it's baking, make the gravy and pan-sear the tuna.

Carrot Raisin Salad

Both adults and kids enjoy this mix of sweet flavours. This recipe yields 12 portions.

2 cups	fat-free plain yogurt	1 cup	raisins
2 tbsp	white sugar	1 cup	drained canned crushed pineapple
½ tsp	ground cinnamon		
8–10	large carrots, cut in chunks		

1. In a small bowl, mix together yogurt, sugar and cinnamon until well blended.
2. Put carrots through the feed tube of a food processor that has been fitted with the shredding blade. Or use a hand grater to shred the carrots. Place in a large mixing bowl.
3. Add raisins and pineapple and blend with a wooden spoon.
4. Pour in yogurt mixture and stir until blended.

Spicy Noodle Salad

Serve this dish at room temperature. This recipe will yield 12 portions.

8 cups	water
2 lb	linguine OR vermicelli
1	medium red pepper, seeded and cut into matchsticks
½ cup	cubed cucumber
4	small bunches green onions (green parts removed), thinly sliced
2 tsp	peanut oil
4 tbsp	sesame seeds

Dressing

6 tbsp	soy sauce
3 tbsp	minced fresh ginger
3 tbsp	rice vinegar
2 tbsp	minced fresh garlic
1 tsp	white sugar
½ tsp	chili powder
6 tbsp	peanut oil
2 tbsp	sesame oil
2 tbsp	chili oil

1. In a medium mixing bowl, make dressing. Whisk together soy sauce, ginger, vinegar, garlic, sugar and chili powder. Gradually add in the peanut, sesame and chili oils, whisking until blended.
2. In a large saucepan, bring water to a boil over high heat. Add the linguine. Reduce heat to medium low and cook for about 7 minutes or until al dente. Drain. Place in large serving bowl.
3. Add red pepper, cucumber and green onions to the bowl. Toss with linguine.
4. Add dressing and toss until thoroughly blended.
5. In a small skillet, heat peanut oil over medium heat. Add sesame seeds and sauté for 2 minutes, or until golden. Sprinkle over noodles.

Focaccia with Onion and Garlic

This dough produces a piece of bread as big as a party-sized pizza. This recipe makes 24 pieces.

1 tsp	white sugar
1 cup	warm water (105–115°F)
1 tbsp	active dry yeast
3½ cups	bread flour
1 tsp	salt
2 tbsp	plus 2 tsp olive oil
1 tbsp	minced fresh garlic
¼ cup	vegetable or low-fat chicken broth
1 small	purple onion, thinly sliced
1 tbsp	poppy seeds
2 tbsp	freshly grated Parmesan cheese

1. Dissolve sugar in warm water. Sprinkle the yeast over top and let stand in a warm place for 8 to 10 minutes or until bubbles appear on top.
2. Place flour and salt in a large mixing bowl. Mix with a wooden spoon.
3. Make a well in the centre of the mixture; add yeast and stir until blended. Add 2 tbsp of the oil and mix until dough forms a ball.
4. Dust work surface and hands with flour and knead the dough for about 3 minutes or until the dough is shiny and elastic. Add more flour if the dough seems sticky.
5. Place dough in a greased large bowl. Cover with a tea towel and let rise until doubled in bulk, about 1 hour.
6. Place dough on a surface that has been dusted with flour. Punch it down. Dust your hands with flour and, with your palm, shape dough into a rectangle. Using a rolling pin, roll dough into a 10- x 15-inch rectangle. With the help of two metal spatulas, place dough onto a jelly-roll pan or cookie sheet that has been sprayed with cooking spray. With your index finger, make random indentations in the dough.
7. Preheat oven to 475°F.
8. Mix garlic and remaining 2 tsp oil together in a small bowl. Spread on the bread with a pastry brush.
9. In a medium skillet, heat broth over medium heat. Sauté onion for 3 minutes or until softened. Spread over bread.
10. Sprinkle poppy seeds and cheese over bread.
11. Bake for 20 minutes or until edges are golden brown.
12. Cut into 24 pieces.

Beef Tenderloin

The tenderloin is the long and particularly tender muscle that runs beneath the ribs. It is the choicest of meat cuts. This recipe serves 12, with 2 cups of gravy.

2	beef tenderloins (each about 3 lb)
1 tbsp	olive oil

Marinade

2 tbsp	minced fresh garlic
1 tbsp	minced fresh rosemary
1 tbsp	Dijon mustard
2 tsp	minced fresh thyme
½ tsp	pepper
2 tbsp	olive oil

Gravy

4 cups	low-fat beef broth
1 cup	dry red wine
1 tsp	tomato paste
2 tbsp	low-fat margarine
2 tbsp	instant blending flour

1. In a small bowl whisk together garlic, rosemary, mustard, thyme and pepper. Gradually whisk in the oil.
2. Place tenderloins in a glass baking dish and pour marinade over top. Cover and refrigerate for a few hours or overnight, turning tenderloins over occasionally.
3. Preheat oven to 375°F.
4. Place oil in a large roasting pan. Place directly on the element of the stove and heat at medium for about 30 seconds. Place the tenderloins in the pan and sauté on all sides for about 5 minutes, or until lightly browned.
5. Remove from heat. Place the tenderloins on a rack in the roasting pan and place in the oven.
6. Bake for 25 to 30 minutes for rare, 35 to 45 minutes for medium rare, 45 to 50 minutes for medium, and 50 to 60 minutes for medium-well meat.
7. To make gravy, in a medium saucepan, heat broth, wine and tomato paste over medium heat. Bring to a boil and then reduce heat to simmer.
8. Remove tenderloins and the rack from the roasting pan.
9. Place the roasting pan on an element at medium heat.
10. Slowly pour the broth mixture into the roasting pan. Stir with a wooden spoon to deglaze the pan, dislodging any browned bits.

11. Pour broth mixture from roasting pan into a large measuring cup. Spoon any fat off the top.
12. In a medium saucepan, heat margarine and flour over low heat. Gradually add broth mixture with a wire whisk. Stir until thoroughly blended. Increase heat to medium high and bring to a boil. Reduce heat to simmer.

Pan-Seared Tuna with Three Relishes

You may substitute swordfish or sea bass for the tuna. This recipe yields 12 buffet-size portions, each about 3 ounces.

6	tuna steaks (each 6 oz)	4 tsp	olive oil
	Salt and pepper	½ cup	cubed shallots
1 tsp	ground red pepper flakes	4 tsp	minced fresh garlic
1½ tsp	ground cumin	½ cup	dry white wine
2 tbsp	lemon juice	2 tsp	balsamic vinegar

1. Place tuna steaks on a large glass dish. Sprinkle both sides of steaks with salt and pepper, red pepper flakes and cumin. Squirt lemon juice over top. Cover and refrigerate for at least 1 hour or overnight.
2. Using two large skillets at the same time, heat 2 tsp of the olive oil in each one over medium heat. Add ¼ cup of the shallots and 2 tsp garlic to each pan and sauté for 1 to 2 minutes or until softened.
3. Push shallots and garlic to one side and add three steaks to each pan. Sauté for 3 to 4 minutes.
4. Flip fish over. Pour ¼ cup of the wine and 1 tsp of the vinegar into each pan. Reduce heat to simmer and cook for an additional 3 to 4 minutes. The fish will be slightly underdone in the centre. For fish that is cooked through, sauté each side for 5 to 7 minutes or until fish flakes easily with a fork and flesh is opaque.
5. Carefully cut each steak in half to create small individual portions.

Relishes on the Side

Use these relishes as pasta sauces, roulade fillings and crostini toppings. Their versatility rules!

Vegie Relish

This recipe yields about 6 cups.

4 cups	cubed tomatoes	½ cup	minced fresh parsley
1 cup	cubed purple onion	¼ cup	minced fresh basil
½ cup	green olives, cut in ½-inch cubes	1 tbsp	minced fresh garlic
½ cup	niçoise olives, cup in ½-inch cubes	2 tsp	lemon juice
		2 tbsp	olive oil

1. In a large mixing bowl, combine tomatoes, onion, green and niçoise olives, parsley and basil.
2. In a small bowl, whisk together garlic and lemon juice. Add oil and blend thoroughly.
3. Pour over tomato mixture and stir until combined.

Don't Hold the Anchovies

This recipe yields about 4 cups.

1½ cups	drained oil-packed sun-dried tomatoes, cut in small pieces	4 tbsp	capers
1½ cups	roasted red peppers (from a jar), cut in small pieces	2 tsp	minced fresh garlic
4–5	anchovies, finely chopped	¼ cup	lemon juice
		1 tsp	Dijon mustard
		½ tsp	Worcestershire sauce
		2 tbsp	olive oil

1. In a large mixing bowl, combine tomatoes, red pepper, anchovies and capers.
2. In a small bowl, whisk together garlic, lemon juice, mustard, and Worcestershire sauce. Add oil and blend thoroughly.
3. Pour over tomato mixture and stir until combined.

NOTE: BECAUSE THIS RELISH HAS A STRONG FLAVOUR, USE IT SPARINGLY.

Black Bean Sauce

This recipe yields about 3 cups.

½ cup	low-fat margarine, melted	¼ cup	soy sauce
¼ cup	brown sugar	1 tsp	red pepper flakes
¼ cup	liquid honey	1 can	(19 oz) black beans, drained

1. In a medium bowl, whisk together margarine, sugar, honey, soy sauce and red pepper flakes.
2. Fold in black beans with a wooden spoon.

Potato Croquettes

Croquettes derive their name from the French verb *croquer* which means "to crunch." They are small patties, usually made from potato, rice, cheese and vegies, that are coated with bread crumbs. This recipe yields about 12 croquettes.

6 cups	boiling water
3 large	potatoes, peeled and cut into chunks
1 tbsp	chopped fresh parsley
1 tbsp	freshly grated Parmesan cheese
1 tsp	minced fresh garlic
1 tsp	chopped chives
1	egg
	Salt and pepper
2 tbsp	all-purpose flour
1	egg white, slightly beaten
½	cups crushed saltine crackers

1. In a large saucepan, bring water to a boil over high heat. Add potato chunks. Reduce heat to medium low and cook for 20 to 25 minutes or until fork tender.
2. Pass potato chunks through a potato ricer and into a large mixing bowl. Add parsley, cheese, garlic, chives and egg. Sprinkle with salt and pepper to taste. Stir with a wooden spoon until completely blended.
3. Shape mixture into small patties using about 2 tbsp mixture per pattie. Dip in flour, egg white and crushed saltines. Place on a sheet of wax paper that has been dusted with cornstarch.
4. In a large skillet, heat oil over medium heat. Add one batch of croquettes and sauté for 3 minutes per side or until lightly browned. Repeat with remaining oil and batches of croquettes.

Zucchini Boats Stuffed with Hummus

This recipe makes 12 little boats.

2	large zucchini
1 tbsp	low-fat margarine, melted
	Salt and pepper

Hummus

2 cups	drained canned chick peas
¼ cup	tahini
Juice of 1	lemon
2 tsp	minced fresh garlic
1 tsp	salt
1 tbsp	olive oil
Pinch	red pepper flakes

1. Preheat oven to 350°F.
2. Cut each zucchini in half lengthwise. Scoop out pulp, leaving about ½ inch intact around outer edges. Brush with margarine. Sprinkle with salt and pepper to taste. Cut each slice into thirds widthwise and place in a baking sheet that has been sprayed with cooking spray.
3. Bake for 20 minutes or until tender.
4. Meanwhile, place the chick-peas, tahini, lemon juice, garlic and salt in the work bowl of a food processor. Process for 15 seconds. Add oil and red pepper flakes and process for another 10 seconds.
5. When zucchini have finished baking, remove from oven and place approximately 1 tbsp of the hummus in each boat.

Bread Pudding

A warm and comforting conclusion to an evening of family interaction. This recipe serves 12.

¼ cup	raisins	2 cups	1% milk
¼ cup	dried cranberries	5	eggs
¼ cup	bourbon **OR** rum	¼ cup	brown sugar
8 cups	cubed challah **OR** baguette	2 tsp	vanilla
		1½ tsp	ground cinnamon
¼ cup	low-fat margarine, melted	¼ cup	white chocolate chips

1. Place raisins and cranberries in a large mixing bowl. Pour bourbon over top. Cover and soak overnight.
2. Preheat oven to 400°F.
3. Place bread cubes in a large mixing bowl. Pour margarine over top and mix thoroughly. Spread out on a cookie sheet and bake for 5 minutes until toasted. Place in large bowl and set aside. Reduce heat to 350°F.
4. Place milk and eggs in another large mixing bowl and beat thoroughly with a wire whisk. Gradually add sugar, vanilla and cinnamon, whisking until thoroughly blended.
5. Add egg mixture to the bowl of bread cubes and mix thoroughly.
6. Pour raisin mixture through a sieve. Add raisins and cranberries to the bread mixture. Add chocolate chips and mix well.
7. Pour bread mixture into a 9- x 13-inch glass baking dish that has been sprayed with cooking spray.
8. Place glass dish inside a large roasting pan. Add water until the water level rises 1 inch up the sides of the dish.
9. Bake for 45 minutes or until a knife inserted comes out clean. Cut into 12.

Meals in a Pot

This fish stew, popular along the French Mediterranean coast, is a meal in itself. This recipe yields about 8 portions.

Easy Bouillabaisse

1 tbsp	olive oil
2	medium potatoes, peeled and cut in ½-inch cubes
2	medium carrots, cut in ½-inch rounds
1	medium green pepper, seeded, and cut into ½-inch cubes
1	medium onion, cut in ½-inch cubes
1 tbsp	minced fresh garlic
1 can	(28 oz) plum tomatoes, undrained
½ cup	dry red wine
2 cups	vegetable broth
1 tsp	lemon juice
¼ tsp	white sugar
Dash of	Tabasco
1	bay leaf
2 lb	red snapper fillets, cut into 2-inch pieces
12	uncooked peeled medium-sized shrimp
12	scallops
2 tbsp	chopped fresh parsley
Salt and pepper	

1. In a large soup pot, heat oil over medium heat. Add potatoes, carrots, green peppers, onion and garlic. Sauté for 5 to 7 minutes or until wilted and golden.
2. Add tomatoes, wine, broth, lemon juice, sugar, Tabasco and bay leaf. Reduce heat to low.
3. Add snapper. Cover and cook for 20 minutes. Add shrimp and scallops. Cover and cook for another 5 minutes or until seafood is cooked through.
4. Discard bay leaf. Add parsley and salt and pepper to taste.

Many Ways for Potatoes

Scalloped Potatoes

Serves 6 to 8

Preheat oven to 375°F. Cut 4 medium potatoes into ¼-inch rounds. Place a layer of potatoes in a 9- x 13-inch baking dish that has been sprayed with cooking spray. Sprinkle with salt and pepper. Repeat layers with remaining slices. In a small saucepan, heat 2 tbsp low-fat margarine over medium-low heat. Whisk in 2 tbsp instant blending flour. Slowly add 1 cup vegetable or low-fat chicken broth and whisk until thoroughly blended. Pour mixture over potatoes. Bake for about 1 hour or until tender.

Mashed Potatoes

Serves 6 to 8

Boil 4 medium potatoes, scoop out the pulp and pass it through a potato ricer into a large mixing bowl. Melt 2 tbsp low-fat margarine and add to potatoes, along with ¼ tsp white pepper, 1 tsp salt and 1 tsp minced fresh garlic (if desired). Microwave ¼ cup 1% milk at medium for 1 minute and add to potatoes. Blend thoroughly with a wooden spoon.

Home Fries

Serves 6 to 8

Bake or broil 4 medium potatoes and cut into ½-inch cubes. Set aside. In a large saucepan, heat 1 tbsp canola oil over medium heat. Cut 1 large onion into ½-inch cubes and sauté, along with 1 tbsp minced fresh garlic. Add potatoes and sauté until heated through. Sprinkle with salt and pepper.

Roasted Potatoes

Serves 6 to 8

Preheat oven to 350°F. Place 3 lb scrubbed, unpeeled, small new potatoes in a 9- x 13-inch glass baking dish that has been sprayed with cooking spray. Sprinkle with salt, pepper and paprika. Drizzle 1 tbsp olive oil over them. Bake for 1 hour or until fork tender.

Potato Skins

Serves 6 to 12

Preheat oven to 425°F. Bake 6 large potatoes and scoop out the pulp, leaving a ¼-inch thick shell for each potato. Brush each cavity with melted low-fat margarine. Sprinkle with salt and pepper and place on a cookie sheet that has been sprayed with cooking spray. Bake for 10 to 12 minutes or until golden. Fill the skins with fat-free sour cream or salsa. Or sprinkle with shredded low-fat cheddar cheese and broil for 2 minutes or until melted.

Chicken Fricassee

After making Baby Drums (p.133), you can use the wing tips from the chicken wings for making this fricassee. This recipe makes 12 portions.

1 tbsp	olive oil
4 lb	chicken parts, cut into small pieces
	Salt and pepper
3	medium onions, thinly sliced
2	medium carrots, cut into ½-inch rounds
1	large potato, cut into ½-inch cubes
1 tbsp	minced fresh garlic
7 cups	low-fat chicken broth
1 cup	dry white wine
3 large	tomatoes, cut into ½-inch cubes
1 tsp	dried thyme
1 tsp	dried oregano
¼ tsp	chili powder

1. In a large soup pot, heat oil over medium heat. Add chicken and sauté for 5 to 7 minutes or until browned. Sprinkle with salt and pepper. Remove from pot and set aside.
2. Add onions, carrots, potato and garlic to pot and sauté for 3 to 5 minutes or until softened.
3. Add broth, wine, tomatoes, thyme, oregano and chili powder to pot. Bring to a boil. Reduce heat to simmer.
4. Return chicken to pot. Cover and simmer for 45 minutes to 60 minutes or until chicken is cooked through and vegetables are tender.

THE SPORTING LIFE

There is a certain pastime in my household that the family enjoys year-round – watching sports on TV. All sports are included but power boat racing, hockey, football and wrestling are the favourites.

Special events, like the Olympic Games, the Stanley Cup, the World Series, the Grey Cup and Wrestlemania, deserve a good food accompaniment. In return for your hard work, ask those sports fans to clean up.

Menu

Serves 12

Cheese Dreams

Pita Chips with Sun-Dried Tomatoes and Mozzarella Cheese

Tortilla Chips with Guacamole and Tomatoes

Cobb Salad

Sweet-Tasting Salmon

Loaded-Up Lasagne

Oven-Baked Rice

Fruit Slices and Dip

Oven-Roasted Pears

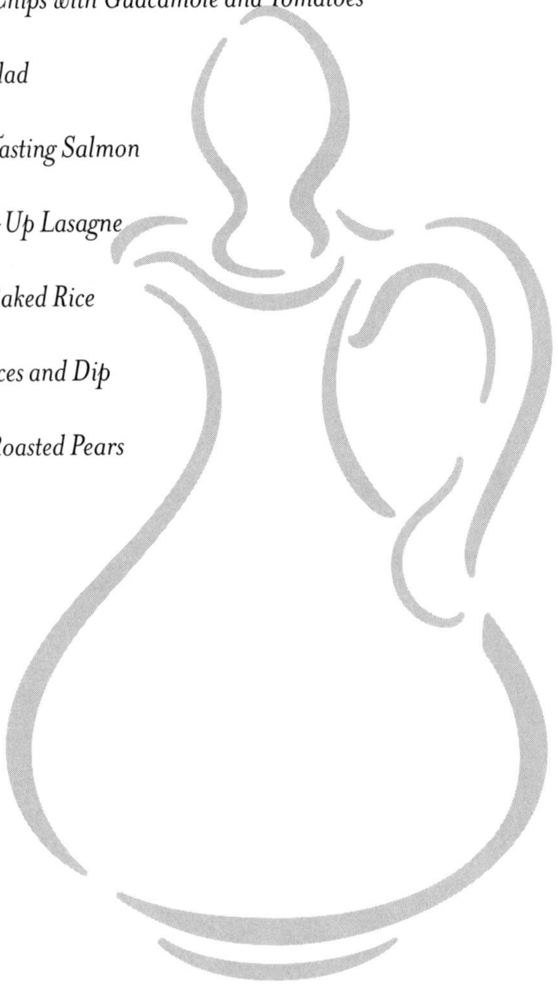

Presentation

Everyday dishes and silverware are perfectly fine for this occasion. It is doubtful that your guests will even notice what they are eating *with* or what they are eating *on*. Lots of napkins, paper towels and garbage bags are in order as the eating will take place in front of the TV. It is probably a good idea for the cook to present the buffet, go to the movies and return when the party is over. Leave signs out in noticeable places suggesting that the clean-up be done promptly by the guests. Be optimistic.

Platters should be used for the salmon, the Tortilla Chips, the Pita Chips, the Cheese Dreams, the Cobb Salad and the Fruit Slices and Dip. Transfer the rice to a serving bowl. Serve the lasagne and the pears in their wicker baskets.

Instead of a centrepiece, fill the empty spots on the table with chocolate bars.

There is no need for music. The TV is blaring!

Preparation Schedule

A Week Before

Make the Loaded-Up Lasagne. Wrap in foil. Place in a large plastic bag and seal with a twist tie. Freeze.

The Day Before

1. Make the Pita Chips. Store in an airtight container.
2. Make the Tortilla Chips. Store in an airtight container.
3. Make the Russian Dressing and refrigerate.
4. Make the ketchup mixture for the Sweet-Tasting Salmon and refrigerate.
5. Make the dip for the Fruit Slices and refrigerate.
6. Put lasagne in refrigerator to thaw overnight.

That Day

1. Prepare the sun-dried tomatoes for the Pita Chips.
2. Make the Guacamole and chop the tomatoes for the Tortilla Chips.
3. Preheat the oven to 350°F.
4. Put the ingredients for the Cobb Salad on a platter. Refrigerate.
5. Prepare the rice and bake it for 1 hour.
6. Assemble the salmon packages.
7. Prepare the Cheese Dreams.
8. Remove the rice from the oven. Raise heat to 375°F.
9. Bake the Cheese Dreams for 12 to 14 minutes.
10. Assemble the Tortilla Chips with Guacamole and Tomatoes and arrange on a platter.
11. Take the Cheese Dreams out of the oven. Raise heat to 400°F. Bake salmon for 30 minutes.
12. Prepare the pears. Take salmon out of the oven.
13. Raise heat to 425°F and bake pears for 35 to 40 minutes.
14. Arrange Fruit Slices and Dip on a platter.
15. Drizzle Russian Dressing over Cobb Salad.
16. Remove pears from oven. Bake lasagne for 15 minutes.
17. Take lasagne out of the oven. Raise heat to 475°F . Assemble Pita chips and bake for 2 minutes.

Cheese Dreams

These little appetizers are heavenly. This recipe yields about 12 little dreams.

1 cup	shredded low-fat cheddar cheese	½ cup	all-purpose flour
¼ cup	stick-type low-fat margarine, softened	1–2 tbsp	1% or 2% milk

1. Preheat oven to 375°F.
2. Place cheese and margarine in a large mixing bowl. Mix together with a fork until well blended.
3. Add flour and milk and whisk until well blended.
4. Roll mixture into small balls, about 1-inch in diameter.
5. Bake on an ungreased cookie sheet for 12 to 14 minutes or until golden.

Pita Chips with Sun-Dried Tomatoes and Mozzarella Cheese

This recipe makes 12 appetizers.

1 tbsp	olive oil
1 tsp	minced fresh garlic
3	Greek-style pitas
1 cup	drained oil-packed sun-dried tomatoes, chopped into small pieces
1 cup	shredded low-fat mozzarella cheese

1. Preheat oven to 475°F.
2. In a small bowl, whisk together olive oil and garlic. Brush mixture on one side of each pita. Cut each pita in quarters.
3. Place pita pieces on a cookie sheet that has been sprayed with cooking spray. Bake for 5 minutes or until crisp.
4. Put ½ tbsp of the tomatoes on each pita piece. Top with ½ tbsp of the cheese.
5. Return pita chips to the oven and bake for 2 minutes or until cheese is bubbly.

Tortilla Chips with Guacamole and Tomatoes

This recipe makes 12 appetizers.

2 large	tomatoes, cut into ¼-inch dice (about 1 cup)
	Salt and pepper

Tortilla Chips

3	corn tortillas (each 6 inches)
1 tbsp	low-fat margarine, melted
	Salt and pepper
	Garlic powder
	Chili powder

Guacamole

2	ripe avocados, halved, pitted and peeled
2 tsp	minced fresh garlic
2 tbsp	lime juice
2 tbsp	prepared salsa
2 tbsp	minced purple onion
1 tbsp	minced fresh cilantro
¼ tsp	chili powder

1. Preheat oven to 475°F.
2. Cut each tortilla in quarters. Brush both sides of each quarter with margarine. Sprinkle both sides with salt, pepper, garlic powder and chili powder.
3. Place on cookie sheet that has been sprayed with cooking spray. Bake for 3 minutes on each side or until crisp.
4. Place all guacamole ingredients in a large mixing bowl. Mix thoroughly with a fork.
5. Place approximately 1 tbsp of the mixture on top of each chip. Top with 1 tbsp of the chopped tomatoes. Sprinkle with salt and pepper.

Cobb Salad

This salad rids the refrigerator of its leftovers. Arrange the ingredients neatly on a platter, or throw them all into a big salad bowl. This recipe yields 12 small portions.

6 cups	torn iceberg lettuce
3 cups	cubed cooked chicken
1 cup	crumbled blue cheese,
2	medium tomatoes, cut in ½-inch dice
1	ripe avocado, halved, pitted, peeled and cut into ½-inch cubes
2	hard-boiled eggs, coarsely chopped

Russian Dressing

1 cup	fat-free mayonnaise
⅓ cup	chili sauce
1 tsp	lemon juice

1. Whisk all dressing ingredients together in a small bowl.
2. Place all salad ingredients in a large salad bowl or on a platter. Toss or drizzle with dressing.

Sweet-Tasting Salmon

Use this dish as your main course for your dinner for 12.

1½ cups	ketchup	
¾ cup	liquid honey	
½ cup	soy sauce	
2 tbsp	minced fresh garlic	
2	salmon fillets (each about 1½ lb)	
	Salt and pepper	
4	lemons, thinly sliced	
4	small onions, thinly sliced	

1. In a medium bowl, whisk together ketchup, honey, soy sauce and garlic.
2. Preheat oven to 400°F.
3. Sprinkle salmon with salt and pepper. Take two sheets of foil, each big enough to wrap one fillet loosely, and spray them with cooking spray. Arrange the slices from one lemon in a row on each sheet. Place the slices from one onion on top of the lemon slices on each sheet.
4. Place the fish fillets on top of these lemon-onion beds. Pour ketchup mixture over the fillets. Top each one with remaining lemon and onion slices. Close up foils loosely.
5. Place foil packages on a cookie sheet. Bake for 30 minutes or until fish flakes easily with a fork and the flesh is opaque.
6. Place on a large platter. Surround with lemons and onions, if desired.

Loaded-Up Lasagne

This reliable old standard is chock-full of goodies. Add minced chicken or lean ground beef to the Roasted Tomato Garlic Sauce for an even heartier lasagne. This recipe makes 12 small servings.

9	oven-ready lasagne noodles
1	bunch spinach, stems removed
1 tsp	olive oil
2 cups	thinly sliced button mushrooms
1	medium onion cut in ½-inch cubes
2 tsp	minced fresh garlic
2 cups	skim milk cottage cheese
½ cup	fat-free plain yogurt
2	egg whites
1	egg
¼ cup	freshly grated Parmesan cheese
2 cups	prepared spaghetti sauce OR Roasted Tomato Garlic Sauce (see p. 39)
1 cup	shredded low-fat mozzarella cheese
2 tbsp	freshly grated Parmesan cheese
2 tbsp	dry breadcrumbs
2 tbsp	minced fresh parsley

1. Preheat oven to 350°F.
2. Soak noodles in cold water. Drain, pat dry and place on paper towels. Set aside.
3. In a vegetable steamer, cook spinach until wilted, 2 to 3 minutes. Rinse under cold water. Squeeze dry and chop.
4. In a large skillet, heat oil over medium heat. Sauté mushrooms, onion and garlic for 2 to 3 minutes or until softened. Add spinach and continue to cook for another minute. Set aside.
5. Place cottage cheese and yogurt in a large mixing bowl. Blend thoroughly with a fork. Add egg whites and egg and stir until blended. Add Parmesan cheese. Add mushroom mixture and stir with a wooden spoon.
6. To assemble lasagne, place three noodles on the bottom of a 9- x 13-inch glass baking dish that has been sprayed with cooking spray.
7. Place one-third of the cheese mixture over the noodles.
8. Pour one-third of the spaghetti sauce over top.
9. Sprinkle one-third of the mozzarella cheese on top of the spaghetti sauce.

10. Repeat layering of noodles, cheese mixture, sauce and mozzarella cheese twice.
11. In a small bowl, mix together Parmesan cheese and breadcrumbs. Sprinkle on top of lasagne. Sprinkle with parsley.
12. Bake for 35 minutes or until golden.

Oven-Baked Rice

This dish starts off on the stove and finishes up in the oven. It yields 12 small servings.

2 tsp	olive oil	½ cup	chopped fresh parsley
2	small bunches green onions (green parts removed), thinly sliced		Salt and pepper
½ cup	thinly sliced mushrooms	6 cups	water OR vegetable broth or low-fat chicken broth
2 tsp	minced fresh garlic	3 cups	wild rice

1. Preheat oven to 350°F.
2. In a large ovenproof saucepan, heat oil over medium heat. Add onions, mushrooms and garlic and sauté for 2 to 3 minutes or until softened. Stir in parsley. Sprinkle with salt and pepper to taste.
3. Add water, raise heat to medium high, and continue to stir until mixture reaches a boil.
4. Stir in rice. Cover. Place saucepan in oven and bake for 1 hour or until tender.

Fruit Slices and Dip

These are also known as dessert crudités. This recipe provides a light dessert for a party of 12.

12	green apple slices
12	tangerine sections
12	strawberries
12	pear slices
12	cantaloup slices
12	pineapple slices

Dip

2 cups	fat-free plain yogurt
2 tbsp	white sugar
1 tsp	lemon juice
½ tsp	ground cinnamon

1. Place dip ingredients in a large mixing bowl and thoroughly blend with a wooden spoon.
2. Arrange fruit attractively on a platter, with the dip in the centre.

Hoagies

The term *hoagie* is a synonym for submarine, a sandwich made from a long roll or piece of French bread, chock-full of meat, cheese and vegetables. Cut each one in half to make 12 portions.

1 tsp	olive oil
½ cup	button mushrooms, thinly sliced
½ cup	green pepper, cut in ½-inch dice
6 tsp	low-fat Italian dressing
6	submarine rolls
6 oz	cooked sliced roast beef or turkey (from the deli)
6 oz	sliced low-fat mozzarella cheese

1. Preheat oven to 350°F.
2. In a medium skillet, heat oil over medium heat. Add mushrooms and green pepper and sauté for 3 minutes. Set aside.
3. Put 1 tsp Italian dressing on the bottom of each of the buns. Top each one with an ounce of roast beef followed by an ounce of mozzarella cheese.
4. Place sandwiches on a cookie sheet that has been sprayed with cooking spray. Bake for 5 minutes until cheese melts and bun is lightly toasted. Transfer to serving platter and cut in half.

Oven-Roasted Pears

These pears offer a light, refreshing end to a meal. This recipe serves 12.

6 tbsp	brown sugar	1 tsp	ground cinnamon
6 tbsp	water	12	Bosc pears, peeled, halved and cored
4 tbsp	calorie-reduced maple syrup		

1. Preheat oven to 425°F.
2. In a medium bowl, whisk together brown sugar, water, syrup and cinnamon.
3. Place pears in two 9- x 11-inch baking dishes. Pour sauce over pears. Bake for 35 to 40 minutes or until pears are fork tender.

Couch Potato Favourites

Everyone has, at some point, leftover chicken in the fridge. Provided it's only a day old, it can wind up as a fajita ingredient. This recipe makes 4 portions.

Fajitas

4	flour tortillas (each 10 inches)
1 cup	diced cooked chicken
½ tsp	chili powder
1 cup	cubed tomatoes
1 cup	store prepared guacamole dip OR Guacamole (p.179)
1 cup	shredded iceberg lettuce
4 tbsp	shredded low-fat cheddar cheese

1. Preheat oven to 350°F.
2. Lay out tortillas on a work surface. In a small bowl, place chicken. Sprinkle chili powder over the chicken and combine. Place ¼ cup of the chicken in the middle of each tortilla.
3. Place ¼ cup of the tomatoes, ¼ cup of the guacamole dip, ¼ cup of the shredded lettuce and 1 tbsp of the cheese in the middle of each tortilla.
4. Roll each tortilla up and wrap in foil.

LEAVING HOME

I can tolerate a few grey hairs and even a few more facial lines. But when I realized that my eldest son was ready to move out of the house to begin university, I basically retreated into a state of disbelief. Now, who did you say must be getting older?

In a sense this event is a celebration – a tribute to the fact that he has reached a certain level of independence, achievement and maturity. But one fact remains evident: he will have to know how to cook.

You'll be delighted to know that all these recipes are simple. The Menu should serve as a reference guide for your student. (There is no preparation schedule.)

Menu

Check individual recipes for number of portions

Student Style Appetizers:

Goat Cheese Toasts

Basic Bruschetta

Nachos 'n' Cheese

Salads:

The Great Greek Salad

Back-at-the-Ranch Salad

Easy Street Soup

The Spud Gets Dressed Up

Student Stir-Fry

Simplified Pizza

Fusilli with Too-Easy Tomato Sauce

Last-Minute Chili

Not Fried Chicken

Uncomplicated Endings:

Skor Bar Pie

Five-Minute Trifle

Banana Dream Pie

Pizza Cookie

Student-Style Appetizers

These appetizers can be enjoyed as a munch in front of the TV or as a post-study snack.

Goat Cheese Toasts

Serves 24

6	slices white or whole-wheat bread
½ cup	plain or herbed goat cheese

1. Preheat oven to broil.
2. Toast bread slices in toaster on light setting.
3. Cut crusts off the bread and cut each slice into quarters.
4. Spread 1 tsp of the goat cheese on each toast piece. Place on a cookie sheet that has been sprayed with cooking spray.
5. Broil for 1 to 2 minutes or until browned.

Basic Bruschetta

Serves 12

2 cups	cubed tomatoes
1	small bunch green onions (green parts removed), thinly sliced
2 tbsp	freshly grated Parmesan cheese
	Pepper
1	baguette (8 oz), cut into 12 slices

Student's Vinaigrette

½ cup	olive oil
3 tbsp	balsamic vinegar
2 tsp	minced fresh garlic
1 tsp	Dijon mustard

1. In a small bowl, mix together vinaigrette ingredients with a wire whisk. Set aside.
2. In a large bowl, mix together tomatoes, onions and cheese with a wooden spoon. Sprinkle with pepper. Add vinaigrette and mix well.
3. Toast bread slices.
4. Spoon equal amounts of the tomato mixture on top of bread slices.

Nachos 'n' Cheese

Serves 12 to 18

1	large bag (454 g) or 1 lb baked tortilla chips
2 cups	prepared salsa
2–3 cups	mixture shredded low-fat cheddar and mozzarella cheeses

1. Preheat oven to 500°F.
2. Place tortilla chips in an ungreased deep-dish pie plate.
3. Pour salsa over top of chips. Sprinkle cheese over top of salsa.
4. Bake for 5 to 10 minutes or until cheese is melted.

Salads

The Great Greek Salad

A standard in anyone's salad repertoire, this one is always a favourite. This recipe yields 6 main-course portions or 12 appetizer portions.

	Double recipe of Student's Vinaigrette (see p. 190)
6 cups	torn romaine lettuce
2	large tomatoes, quartered
1 cup	crumbled feta cheese
½ cup	pitted black olives
⅓	medium English cucumber, thinly sliced

Combine all ingredients in a salad bowl and toss thoroughly.

Back-at-the-Ranch Salad

This recipe makes 6 main-course portions or 12 appetizer portions. The dressing can double as a pasta sauce for 1 pound of pasta.

6 cups	torn lettuce (romaine, iceberg or a mixture such as mesclun)
6 cups	assorted, cut-up raw vegetables (red peppers, celery, carrots, cucumbers) or leftover cooked vegies

Ranch Dressing

1 cup	buttermilk
¾ cup	fat-free mayonnaise
¼ cup	chopped fresh parsley
1 tsp	minced fresh garlic

Whisk together dressing ingredients in a medium bowl. Place lettuce and vegetables in a large salad bowl. Add dressing and toss thoroughly.

Easy Street Soup

All this soup requires is that your student can boil water. This recipe makes 6 to 8 servings.

7 cups	boiling water
1 bag	(10 oz) frozen peas and carrots
1 pkg	(10 oz) frozen chicken tortellini
6 cups	vegetable or low-fat chicken broth.

1. In a medium saucepan, bring 3 cups of the water to a boil over medium-high heat. Add peas and carrots and follow package directions. Set aside.
2. In another medium saucepan, bring remaining 4 cups water to a boil over medium-high heat. Add tortellini and cook according to package directions. Set aside.
3. In a large saucepan, bring broth to a boil over medium-high heat. Reduce heat to simmer. Add peas and carrots and tortellini and heat through.

The Spud Gets Dressed Up

Eating baked potatoes is an inexpensive and easy way to get vitamin C and potassium into your diet.

Baked Potatoes

Scrub skins thoroughly and prick potatoes with a fork. Place potatoes directly on the oven rack and bake in preheated 425°F oven for about 1 hour or until they yield easily to light pressure.

Toppings:

relish
salsa
shredded low-fat Swiss, mozzarella or cheddar cheese
Dijon, honey or Russian-style mustard
Tabasco
sautéed onions, mushrooms and/or zucchini
broccoli and melted cheddar cheese
chopped fresh herbs
chili powder
leftover chili
leftover vegies
cottage cheese
fat-free sour cream or yogurt
smoked salmon slices
capers
olives
pimentos
anchovies
horseradish

Student Stir-Fry

If your student doesn't own a wok, this dish can be made in a 12-inch skillet. This recipe yields 4 portions.

2 tbsp	soy sauce
1 tbsp	lemon juice
2 tsp	minced fresh garlic
1 tsp	minced fresh ginger
1 tsp	brown sugar
2 tsp	olive oil
¼–½ lb	flank steak, cut in strips
1	large carrot, cut into ½-inch rounds
1	medium red pepper, seeded and cut into match sticks
1	small bunch green onions (green parts removed), thinly sliced
½ cup	low-fat chicken broth
1 tsp	cornstarch
1 tbsp	water

1. In a small bowl, whisk together soy sauce, lemon juice, garlic, ginger and sugar. Set aside.
2. In the large skillet or wok, heat oil over medium heat. Add steak, carrots, red pepper and green onions and sauté 5 to 7 minutes or until steak is browned.
3. Add soy sauce mixture and cook for another 2 to 3 minutes.
4. Reduce heat to low. Add chicken broth. Cover and cook for 1 to 2 minutes longer or until heated through.
5. In a small bowl, whisk together cornstarch and water.
6. Add cornstarch mixture to skillet and sauté for another couple of minutes or until liquid has thickened.

Simplified Pizza

Sometimes it just takes too long for the pizza delivery person to arrive. This pizza provides dinner for 2 or a snack for 4 to 6. Refer to Other Pizza Tops and Bottoms (p. 48) for suggested pizza toppings.

1	prepared pizza crust (11 oz)
¼ cup	prepared pizza sauce
1½–2 cups	shredded low-fat mozzarella cheese

1. Preheat oven to 400°F.
2. Place pizza crust on a pizza pan that has been sprayed with cooking spray. Spread sauce over top. Sprinkle with cheese. Bake for 10 minutes or until cheese is bubbly.

Fusilli with Too-Easy Tomato Sauce

For a heartier sauce, add half a pound of sautéed lean ground beef. This recipe serves 4.

1 tsp	olive oil
¼ cup	chopped onion
2 tsp	minced fresh garlic
1 can	(19 oz) plum tomatoes, undrained
1 tbsp	tomato paste
1 tsp	white sugar
½ tsp	salt
½ tsp	red pepper flakes
4 cups	water
1 lb	fusilli

1. In a large saucepan heat oil over medium heat. Add onions and garlic and sauté for 3 to 5 minutes or until softened.
2. Reduce heat to medium low. Add tomatoes, tomato paste, sugar, salt and red pepper flakes. Cover and simmer until sauce is thick, about 1 hour. Stir occasionally.
3. While sauce is simmering, in a large saucepan bring water to a boil. Add fusilli and cook until al dente, about 7 minutes.
4. Drain. Rinse under cold water and drain.
5. Place pasta in a large bowl and top with sauce.

Last-Minute Chili

It may be a good idea to make a double batch of Too-Easy Tomato Sauce (p.197), so that one batch could be used as the base for this chili. This recipe yields 4 to 6 portions.

1 tsp	canola oil
1 lb	lean ground beef
1 recipe	Too-Easy Tomato Sauce (p. 197)
1 tsp	chili powder
1 can	(14 oz) red kidney beans, drained

1. In a large saucepan, heat oil over medium heat. Add ground beef and sauté until beef is no longer pink, 5 to 7 minutes, breaking up large pieces with a wooden spoon.
2. Add tomato sauce to the saucepan. Sprinkle with chili powder. Bring to a boil, stirring constantly.
3. Reduce heat to low. Add kidney beans. Cover and simmer for another 20 minutes or until beans are heated through.

Not Fried Chicken

This recipe makes 4 portions. Serve this chicken with Fusilli with Too-Easy Tomato Sauce (p.197) and the Great Greek Salad (p.191) for a complete meal.

2 tbsp	Dijon mustard
1 tsp	minced fresh garlic
1 tsp	dried herbs (e.g., basil or rosemary)
1 cup	Italian-style breadcrumbs
1 cup	cornflake crumbs
4	boneless skinless chicken breasts (about 1 lb)
	Salt and pepper

1. Preheat oven to 350°F.
2. In a small bowl, whisk together mustard, garlic and dried herbs. Set aside.
3. In a medium bowl, combine breadcrumbs with cornflake crumbs. Set aside.
4. Sprinkle chicken breasts with salt and pepper.
5. With a pastry brush, spread mustard mixture on each side of each piece of chicken.
6. Dip each piece in crumb mixture and place in a 9- x 13-inch glass baking dish that has been sprayed with cooking spray. Cover with foil.
7. Bake for 20 to 25 minutes. Remove foil cover. Flip breasts over and bake, uncovered, for an additional 20 to 25 minutes or until the chicken is no longer pink inside.

Uncomplicated Endings

By using prepared ingredients in these recipes (angel food cake, graham cracker crumb crusts, pudding, whipped topping), the student gets a head start in the preparation.

Skor Bar Pie

Serves 8 to 12

½ cup	low-fat cream cheese	4	Skor chocolate bars, broken into small pieces
½ cup	1% milk		
2 tsp	vanilla		
1 cup	whipped topping	1	graham cracker crumb pie crust (9 inch)

1. Place cream cheese, milk and vanilla in a large mixing bowl. With an electric mixer, beat at high speed for 2 to 3 minutes or until blended.
2. With a wooden spoon, add whipped topping and mix until thoroughly blended. Add Skor bar pieces.
3. Pour mixture into pie crust and refrigerate for at least 2 hours before serving. Cut into 8 to 12 pieces.

Five Minute Trifle

Serves 8 to 12

1 cup	fresh raspberries	3	containers (each 6 oz) fat-free vanilla yogurt
1 cup	fresh blueberries	6 tbsp	raspberry jam
1 cup	freshly sliced peaches	½ cup	mini chocolate chips
1	angel food cake, cut into 1-inch cubes		

1. In a large bowl, mix together first raspberries, blueberries and peaches. Set aside.
2. Place one-third of the angel food cake cubes on the bottom of a 2-quart glass serving bowl.
3. Cover cubes with one container of the yogurt.
4. Cover the yogurt with one-third of the fruit mixture.
5. Cover fruit mixture with 2 tbsp of the jam.
6. Repeat layers of the cake cubes, yogurt, fruit mixture and jam twice. Sprinkle chocolate chips over top.
7. Refrigerate for at least two hours before serving. Cut into 8 to 12 pieces.

Banana Dream Pie

Serves 8 to 12

4	containers (each 5 oz) fat-free banana pudding
2	large bananas, thinly sliced
2 cups	fat-free sour cream
1	graham cracker crumb pie crust (9 inch)

1. In a large bowl, mix the pudding and bananas with a wooden spoon. Add sour cream and mix until blended.
2. Pour into pie crust and refrigerate for at least 2 hours before serving. Cut into 8 to 12 pieces.

Pizza Cookie

Serves 12 to 16

1 pkg	(18 oz) refrigerated cookie dough
1 cup	whipped topping
1 cup	mini chocolate chips

1. Pat down dough to cover a pizza pan that has been sprayed with cooking spray. Bake according to package directions.
2. When cookie has cooled, spread whipped topping over top. Sprinkle with chocolate chips.
3. Cut into 12 to 16 pieces with a pizza cutter.

Getting Started

Here is a listing of items needed to start the student on a new culinary life.

Kitchen Equipment and Utensils

- 8-inch skillet with nonstick surface (for omelettes, grilled cheese sandwiches and French toast)
- 12-inch skillet (for stir-fries)
- 1-quart enamel saucepan with a lid (for heating soup, boiling eggs)
- 2-quart enamel saucepan with a lid (for Kraft dinner, boiling vegies)
- 6-quart enamel saucepan with a lid (for chili, pasta, soup)
- 2-quart microwaveable glass casserole dish with a lid (for rice)
- 9- x 13-inch glass baking dish with wicker container for serving
- 11- x 13-inch glass baking baking dish with wicker container for serving
- 2 cookie sheets
- pizza pan
- cutting board
- set of mixing bowls
- 4-cup glass measuring cup
- set of dry measuring cups and spoons
- knives:
  - 2 paring knives
  - 1 chef's knife
  - 1 serrated bread knife
  - 1 carving knife
- food processor (optional)
- electric hand mixer
- coffee maker
- kettle
- toaster oven
- pot holders
- corkscrew, bottle opener
- can opener
- set of wooden spoons
- 2 rubber spatulas, 1 metal or plastic spatula
- colander or wire mesh strainer
- kitchen tongs
- hand grater
- soup ladle
- garlic press
- salt shaker, pepper mill

Filling the Pantry

A well-stocked pantry eliminates the need for take-out – almost.

canned chicken broth, canned plum tomatoes, tomato paste
breadcrumbs, cornflake crumbs
olive oil, canola oil
balsamic, red wine and white vinegars
soy sauce, Tabasco
pizza sauce, honey
ketchup, regular and Dijon mustards
calorie-reduced peanut butter, jam, maple syrup
all-purpose flour, white sugar, cornstarch
vanilla, chocolate chips
salt, pepper
dried basil, oregano, rosemary and chili powder
coffee, tea, hot chocolate

In the Fridge

butter or margarine
milk
eggs
fat-free mayonnaise
low-fat cream cheese, yogurt, sour cream
Parmesan cheese
shredded low-fat mozzarella cheese
assorted fruit, vegies, juices

Easy Centrepieces

When you want to put something on the table that is attractive, creative and inexpensive, try one of these suggestions.

1. Line a small wicker basket with a cloth napkin and fill the basket with mandarin oranges.
2. Select from a number of everyday vases – highball glasses, pop bottles, wine bottles, olive oil bottles, ice cream sundae bowls, teapots, pitchers and coffee mugs. Hold flowers together in one hand; cut stems to the desired length with the other hand. If necessary, bundle the stems together with a twist tie.
3. Fill these vases with everyday items other than flowers – breadsticks, asparagus spears, celery stalks, dried spaghetti or linguine, cinnamon sticks, pussywillows, pot-pourri, marbles.
4. Cut the stems of flowers such as daisies or orchids very short. Fill a shallow serving dish with an inch or two of water. Sprinkle with a couple of drops of food colouring. Float the flowers in the water.
5. Draw a face on a pumpkin with magic markers.
6. Float candles in highball glasses.
7. Group together a few small pots of African violets, home-grown herbs or cacti.
8. Fill a serving platter with gourds.
9. Surround a large leafy cabbage with yellow, orange and green peppers.
10. Place a stuffed animal, doll or piggy bank between two candlesticks.
11. Secure three helium balloons with long, colourful ribbons to the table with a large paperweight.
12. Fill a shallow wicker bread basket with small jars. Fill each jar with a small bundle of flowers. Hide any exposed parts of the jars with ivy.
13. Place a piece of water-soaked floral foam in a soup bowl. Stick three toothpicks in the bottom of a candle and insert it into the foam. Insert a mixture of ivy and fresh herbs (green and purple basil, lavender, thyme and sage) into the foam to surround the candle. Let some of the leaves cascade onto the table.

INDEX